D0434935

We Are Arrested

We Are Arrested

A JOURNALIST'S NOTES FROM A TURKISH PRISON

Can Dündar

Biteback Publishing

First published in Great Britain in 2016 by
Biteback Publishing Ltd
Westminster Tower
3 Albert Embankment
London SE1 7SP
Copyright © Can Dündar 2016

Originally published as *Tutuklandık* in Turkey in 2016 by Can Yayınları
© Kalem Agency

ISBN 978-1-78590-138-6

10 9 8 7 6 5 4 3 2 1

A CIP catalogue record for this book is available from the British Library.

Set in Arno Pro by Adrian McLaughlin

Printed and bound in Great Britain by
CPI Group (UK) Ltd, Croydon CR0 4YY

CONTENTS

FOREWORD

ON 6 May 2016, as I was leaving the house in the morning, I noticed something strange.

My bodyguard, who had been my constant companion for a while, wasn't in the car that had come to collect me. He had been officially appointed in the face of increasing threats; but for some reason, he had overslept that morning.

Yet, it was an important day. The court would announce the judgment on the case in which we faced two life sentences.

I rang him and asked him to come to court. He did.

We entered the chamber, quiet due to the order banning the public. We made our closing statements, reiterating that sentencing a news item whose veracity was proven and whose value to the public was evident would damage press freedom and trample on justice.

The judge took a recess before announcing his decision.

We went out. As we were leaving the courthouse to wait at

the café nearby, I noticed the bodyguard was – for whatever reason – absent once again. I was with my wife and a CHP MP, chatting to fellow journalists waiting at the exit when I spotted a sinister face rushing towards me.

I saw the glint of the barrel first and smelled the discharged bullet. And heard him shout 'Traitor!' at the same time. This was the term President Erdoğan was trying to ascribe to me. The bullet had to be the 'heavy price' he wanted me to pay...

This was supposedly the most secure plaza in Turkey: 'Not a bird would be allowed to fly,' as the saying goes, never mind enter carrying a weapon. As the TV reporter shielded me, my wife reacted quite by instinct, grabbing the assailant by the arm as the MP seized him by the throat.

Plainclothesmen got to the scene just then and arrested the gunman. My fellow journalist sustained a minor graze on the leg; I got off lightly thanks to the heroism of those around me. But it was now evident that the threat wasn't just to my newspaper, journalism or freedom. Now my own life was under threat.

Soon afterwards, parting a group of friends who had rushed over at news of the attack, we entered the courtroom for the decision.

The judge started with, 'Sorry about the attack,' before passing sentence: 'Five years and ten months' imprisonment for divulging state secrets.'

As we left the courthouse, I said, 'In the space of an hour, we have experienced two assassination attempts, one physical, the other judicial,' and added that we would never be silenced.

The gunman later said in his initial statement that his aim was to scare me over the news report I had published. The court returned my passport on the same day it passed the custodial sentence.

Did they mean to say, 'Stay away from this country'?

As this book goes to print, the decision of the Court of Appeal is still pending. The prison sentence hangs on our necks, and the smell of gunpowder is etched in our minds.

* * *

2016 was one of the most traumatic years in my life, but also in the history of Turkey. Precisely ten weeks after me, Turkish democracy also faced a grave armed attack.

On 15 July, the Gülen congregation that had partnered the government for many years attempted a coup. There was a mutiny in the army: Parliament was bombed, troops fought the police and, in some areas, troops fought troops. Despite the enormous amount of blood that was spilt, thankfully this armed attempt failed.

The Turkish public had suffered so much under coups throughout history; this time, they went out into the squares and lay before tanks to save the country from a terrible catastrophe.

Sadly, in the aftermath of this brutal attempt, the Turkish government chose to increase oppression rather than channel this opportunity for solidarity against a coup. A state of emergency was declared. The European Convention of Human Rights was suspended. The government assumed Rule by Decree, effectively bypassing Parliament. Detention periods were extended. A campaign was launched to reinstate the death penalty. In a countrywide witch-hunt, thousands of journalists, writers, academics, judges, prosecutors, soldiers, police officers and civil servants were arrested. Dozens of newspapers and websites were closed down, and others were intimidated. Western reaction to these measures strained relations even more and things now appear to have come to a breaking point.

The military coup was foiled, but a civilian coup had suspended freedoms.

* * *

As for the personal consequences of the coup…

The first officials to be dismissed in the higher ranks of the judiciary were Constitutional Court judges who had ordered our release. Then the entire structure of the Court of Appeals that was due to debate our appeal to the prison sentence was changed. The prosecutor who had asked for our detention and authored the indictment has been appointed as the Chief Prosecutor of Istanbul. A new case has been filed, claiming that by running the original news item that had caused my detention, I had assisted the Gülen organisation alleged to have engineered the coup attempt. And the court that filed this case ordered the cancellation of my passport even before the hearings had begun.

2016 had started in a prison cell; halfway through the year, it continues with the smell of gunpowder, prison sentences, new court cases and the possibility of another arrest.

Just like me, Turkey's feeble democracy tries to find a way out, to breathe and create hope for the future amongst the coup attempts, witch-hunts, arrest campaigns and oppressive policies.

* * *

Every sentence written on a country in which everything changes by the day is sentenced to grow old rapidly... All the same, I would like to be able to read these lines under better conditions tomorrow, to be able to say, 'Those were dark times; they're gone now,' as we document the era this book was written in.

As we present *We Are Arrested* to European readers, I would like to call out not only as a journalist fighting for the freedom of the press, but also as the citizen of a nation trying to sustain democracy on a perilous pendulum swinging between the barracks and the mosque:

Support the struggle for existence fought by Turkey's democratic powers.

This support is as crucial to Europe as it is to Turkey.

A Turkey without Europe will turn into an excluded, anti-Western, totalitarian country; but a Europe without Turkey will turn into an equally monochromatic, insular and ineffective continent.

Convince Turkey that Europe is not a Christian club, that it is a partnership of contemporary principles, and Europe will be able to defeat the increasing threat of Islamophobia by embracing the most secularist country in the Muslim world.

That is the only way to stop this dirty war tainting Islam with terrorism and the reaction that has triggered an escalating ultra-nationalism in the West.

Can Dündar
September 2016

PREFACE

ONE DAY, the hatch in my cell door opened. The warder shouted, 'Can Dündar! You have a special visitor.'

'A special visitor?' Not a term I'd heard before.

I had a total of 350 visitors during my three months in Silivri. Lawyers with permanent passes, MPs with Ministry of Justice permits and friends and family who came on visit days. However, in a departure from standard practice, the ministry had refused every single special visit request – and there had been hundreds. No exceptions had been made to date: no foreign delegation, no professional organisation and most certainly not a single colleague…

That day was the only exception.

Someone had applied to the ministry and had somehow succeeded in obtaining permission for a special visit. I nearly broke into a run to reach the large open visit hall. It was empty. I sat down at one of the plastic tables. Staring at the photograph of the free horses as usual, I wondered who my special visitor was. It wasn't long before the door opened. Anticipation was building, as if awaiting the big reveal of a matchmaking show.

And...

Can Öz stepped in, a heart-warming, bearded smile on his face. I couldn't believe my eyes. However he'd managed it, he had broken through strict solitary, and here he was, on an open visit.

I asked, 'How come? How did you get permission?' as we hugged. He told me that Can Publishing's solicitor Ümit Altaş had personally applied to the Ministry of Justice in Ankara, asserting that a face-to-face meeting between publisher and author was essential to discuss copyright and contracts etc.

As far as I can make it out, once business matters came into play, that was that – permission was granted at once. We chatted non-stop throughout the hour, which flew by. We talked of the oppression in the country, the new editions of my books, of new books, and of his daughter, who would be born any day now. My trial had led me to deliberate about publishing my Master's paper on state secrets. I had it with me; except, having been written twenty years earlier, it was now quite obsolete in content. Updating it would require a serious amount of work, which would have been quite a challenge to tackle inside. I had changed my mind. That being said, I was writing all the time. This had probably been the most productive three months of my life…

I had finished the text of the interrupted Cuba documentary. I had submitted numerous articles to leading newspapers of the world, and not just to *Cumhuriyet*. I had managed to whizz off messages to the Vigil of Hope, to award ceremonies, to professional organisations and foreign statesmen. I had replied to each and every letter I'd received. And I was regularly keeping a diary; creating the infrastructure of a book I would write in the future.

It was around then, in January 2016, that *Hürriyet*'s[1] Ertuğrul Özkök heralded a new memoir that would soon join the Silivri anthology: 'The most emotional book's on the way.'

True enough, Silivri memoirs filled several shelves in my bookcase. Some – like Nedim Şener's,[2] for instance – suggested there was little need to write about similar incidents and emotions, and I had mentally shelved my own.

As Can Öz and I chatted, however, I noticed his excitement at my notes, my Silivri memories and the book on my mind. I realised writing it would keep me fit inside. It would also be a testimony; documenting a period of tyranny and the prison that has come to symbolise it — the diary of a captive, a letter from a desert island.

I sent Can off with a hug and returned to my cell. Pulling up a blank notebook, I began to write.

* * *

This is the first book I have ever written in longhand. I was allowed neither a computer nor a typewriter in Silivri Prison. I hadn't written anything in longhand since secondary school. When I was a kid, I wanted to be a doctor. I never made it, or, rather, only got as far as the illegible handwriting. Given that the manuscript would be all but indecipherable to anyone else, I had to write it in capitals and in a legible hand.

My hand tired easily, which showed, so I needed frequent breaks to shake off the pins and needles and rest my arm. My left hand was briefly enlisted to help, but it lacked the skill to cope. It took two months of persistence, but permission to use the computer for an hour twice a week eventually came through, by which time the book was nearly done. At any rate, editorial input from prison administration that inspected the printouts was not required.

This book was planned during long sessions of exercise, staring at the panorama of yellow walls, on the iron bed of the upper bunk in the cell and right next to the radiator on the lower.

I wasn't swayed by the idea of publishing it as a diary; instead, I gathered my memories in chronological order under pithy headings.

I sat in a plastic chair with a white cushion of blanket

material and wrote on a white plastic table with a vinyl cover. It's often said that the best books are always written facing the most magnificent views. I found it's quite the opposite… Imagination stultified by magnificent views occasionally soars to see what lies beyond when it meets a wall. It climbs the wall as it whips up the pen to keep up.

It took me two months, three ballpoint pens and three ruled notebooks to write *We Are Arrested*; at times feeling sad, but mostly with a smile, and always sitting down at the table with a great deal of enthusiasm, dreaming of the day of publication…

My tweet at the time of the court order marked not only the start of our imprisonment, but also the increasingly heavy and extended social servitude under AKP[3] rule. We may even have been the luckiest internees of that long servitude… Ours could only be counted as training in comparison to thousands of victims imprisoned unjustly for years, who lost their lives as they fought for justice or were forgotten in some corner of a dungeon.

Nevertheless, given my pen's long range, and its power to touch hearts and reach a loyal readership, I had a responsibility to those still inside to record, document, announce and scream this injustice for posterity.

* * *

The trial date was as yet unknown at the time of Can's visit; the one thing we did know, though, was that his baby was due at the end of March. I had set my heart on 30 March for publication as a little gift on the occasion of his becoming a father. Then our trial date was set as 25 March. The two dates practically coincided. The book might come out before me, telling the whole world about my circumstances. Thankfully, that's not what happened; I was released before 25 March and wrote the final chapters outside of prison, facing a magnificent view.

This book is the product of a collective act of solidarity.

With Cinnamon in Seferihisar

I would like to thank my wife Dilek, who tirelessly fetched books from my library, offered advice and raised my morale; my comrade Erdem, who shared the pains of the writing process; Tahir Özyurtseven and Murat Sabuncu, who gave me the time to finish the book despite the months of exhaustion; Akın Atalay, who was the first person to read it and caution me to avoid even further trouble; Özlem Yılmaz, who deciphered that awful scrawl, found appropriate visuals and made suggestions about the content; my dear editors Sırma Köksal and Emre Taylan, who never abandoned me throughout court and prison; Utku Lomlu, who proved his graphic design genius once more by enriching literature with a new device (prison bars made out of a hashtag in the original edition); my lawyer friend Ümit Altaş, who built a bridge to my publisher; and my assistant Ayçin Yenitürk, who helped fill in the blanks in the book initially encouraged by Can Öz.

* * *

The fury raging through the palace and the pool media at our release suggests this book is not yet finished. We anticipate new, increased oppression for future memoirs. The more they oppress, the higher our print run. Only time will tell which one will eventually prevail: government oppression or the book's print runs.

CAN DÜNDAR
March 2016

1

CRIME

Thursday 28 May 2015, 3 p.m.

AN EMERGENCY meeting took place on the fifth floor of
Cumhuriyet, in the office where İlhan Selçuk had worked for
a while. It was made even stuffier – heavy as lead – once the
bulletproof blinds were drawn. There were seven of us: four
journalists from editorial – Tahir Özyurtseven, Murat Sabuncu,
Doğan Satmış and I – and three lawyers facing us – Akın Atalay,
Bülent Utku and Abbas Yalçın. Hikmet Çetinkaya joined us later.

On the agenda was an image, and the image was of a
crime… It wasn't my crime; but I would be accused. Because
I had taken the decision to publish that image.

The video from which the image in question was taken

showed an articulated lorry belonging to the MİT, the National Intelligence Agency, intercepted by the gendarmerie. An altercation ensues between the agents and the gendarmes. The gendarmes insist the agents leave the vehicle, and then carry out a search under a warrant from the prosecutor. The steel doors open to reveal boxes of medicines placed as camouflage over the heavy artillery underneath: mortar rounds, grenade launchers, etc.

The footage was recorded on 19 January 2014. Sixteen months had gone by; the matter was raised in the press, in the judiciary and Parliament, and had been debated and criticised. The government had been all but caught red-handed at a time of intensified allegations of supporting Al Qaeda and aiding ISIS militants. This was Turkey's Irangate.

Earlier official claims of humanitarian aid had collapsed. The Turkmens themselves had refuted the defence: 'We were shipping weapons to the Turkmens.'

The prosecutors who had ordered the interception of the lorries had talked, the statements had been leaked and the photos had circulated. What was new was the video. The footage shot by the gendarmerie left no room for doubt since it documented the goods in transit. This was nothing less than an international scandal – and the election was just around the corner.

Cumhuriyet had been chasing the matter for some time. Ahmet Şık[4] had met the suspended prosecutor Aziz Takçı on

8 March 2015, and we had carried the story on the front page. We could feel we were getting really close to the images of the raid itself.

Finally, on the afternoon of Wednesday 27 May, a leftist MP friend delivered the video.

'What you want to know is on this flash drive,' he said. It dispelled all my doubts: MİT was shipping arms to Syria.

A newspaper editor receives numerous tips and documents every day. At the time, you doubt their veracity or the motivation of the bearer. The risk of being manipulated for some purpose or another is quite high. That's when you ask yourself two questions: is this document genuine, and would it be in public interest to publish it? If the answer to both is 'yes' then hiding it in a drawer instead of publishing it is a betrayal of your profession.

We would publish, without a shadow of a doubt. Since it was quite late, however, we agreed to postpone by a day. The next morning, we set about designing the front page on a computer in the far corner of the fourth floor; only a handful knew about this material. We picked the clearest stills and positioned them on the page. The headline documented a lie: 'The weapons denied by Erdoğan!'

That's when it occurred to me to apprise Akın Atalay of our bombshell. His position as our CEO made him the overall boss of the newspaper on behalf of the Cumhuriyet

Foundation. He was scrupulous about preserving the fine line between the editorial opinion and the foundation's. He was the newspaper's solicitor as well as my own and I habitually consulted him on such sensitive news.

When he watched the footage, the journalist in him leapt to his feet in excitement, and then the lawyer's call to sobriety made him sit back down. 'Have you considered the repercussions?' he asked.

Alarm bells rang. That was how we convened the emergency meeting on 28 May, in which journalists and lawyers sat facing one another on black leather armchairs.

The veteran *Cumhuriyet* legal team knew journo-speak; in cases like this they would explain the risks and leave the decision with the editorial team, which is exactly what they did on this occasion.

Akın was quite clear as he opened the meeting: 'They will claim this was a state secret. They've already arrested the prosecutors and the troops who had intercepted the lorries. Disclosing state secrets is a serious crime. Detention is inevitable. I'm personally not against publishing, but I must point out the risks. Please keep this in mind.'

I turned to Bülent Utku, the experienced lawyer in our defence team.

'The risk is high, Can,' he said. 'I'd recommend not publishing.'

'I say we publish,' interrupted assistant editor-in-chief Tahir.

'Except, if Can's going to be the one to pay, it has to be his own decision.'

Our news coordinator Murat was of the view that, with a week to go before the election on 7 June, no one would touch *Cumhuriyet* or me.

Akın said, 'Erdoğan could do anything.'

Murat's suggestion, 'What if we all signed it, and published with joint signatures?', met Doğan's objection: 'That would make us look like an organisation, not journalists.'

'Upload the video on YouTube?'

'Could be construed as fraud.'

We decided it was best to be transparent, open and honest. We were convinced we were committing no crime; quite the opposite, we were about to expose one.

Having assumed an authority it did not have, the intelligence agency was shipping weapons to a neighbouring country without parliamentary sanction, destined, in all likelihood, for radical Islamist organisations. This made Turkey a party in the Syrian civil war. The public had a right to know this, and vote accordingly in the election. They would be the ones to pay the price, after all.

By a strange coincidence, the Master's paper I'd written at the Middle Eastern Technical University was about state secrets and freedom of the press. I was well versed in the regulations and case studies from around the world. I knew that crimes could not be kept secret. One after the other, files stamped *Top Secret* concealing dirty operations sanctioned by politicians had been exposed: Watergate, Irangate, the Pentagon Papers and WikiLeaks being just a handful of examples. And in each case, it was the guilty politicians who were tried, not the journalists. We had a powerful news item and my conscience was clear. It was in the public interest to bring this to light. We could defend it.

'What's the worst-case scenario?' I asked.

'They could raid the newspaper at night, seize the papers and arrest you,' warned the lawyers.

'All right, then we run with it,' I said.

Their apprehension on my account was palpable. I appreciated their concern, but this was a time for information, not apprehension.

There was one last suggestion as the meeting broke up: 'All right; you won't change your mind. But don't risk being arrested at least. Go abroad.'

'When?' I asked.

'At once. Now.'

The election was ten days away. It looked unlikely that the government would raid the most prestigious newspaper in the country just as we were about to go to the polls. But you never knew with Erdoğan. It made sense to mind our step until the election and evaluate developments afterwards.

We took several decisions:

Firstly, we would run teasers on the website, '*Cumhuriyet* has a bombshell' and the like, but wait until morning to run the story.

Emergency editorial meeting, *l to r*: Hikmet Çetinkaya, Murat Sabuncu, Can Dündar, Tahir Özyurtseven, Akın Atalay, Bülent Utku, Doğan Satmış and Abbas Yalçın

Secondly, we wouldn't run it in the early editions of the paper that went to the provinces in order to minimise the risk of a raid on the print shop. Thirdly, I would write a leader explaining to the readers why we were publishing.

NEDEN YAYIMLIYORUZ?

Patlaması halinde bir şehri yok edecek kadar çok silah, bu ülkenin hava limanına gizlice indiriliyorsa,

O silahlar TIR'lara yüklenip bu ülkenin şehirlerinden, topraklarından, sınırlarından geçiriliyorsa,

O silahlar, o ülkenin bütün denetim kurumlarından, idari yetkililerinden, halkından habersizce, komşudaki bir savaşın taraflarından birine destek olmak için gönderiliyorsa,

Gönderilen taraf, bu ülkenin sınırları içinde silahlı eylem yapmış, bu ülkeyi sık sık tehdit etmiş, vahşi bir terör örgütüyse,

Gönderen hükümet, bu silahların mevcudiyetini ısrarla reddediyor, bu silahları durduran askeri yetkilileri görevden aldırıyor, bu silahlar hakkında soruşturma açan savcıları tutuklatıyor, yargılatıyorsa,

Bu ülkenin halkı, bu silahlar dolayısıyla karşı karşıya olduğu riskleri bilmiyor, bu sevkıyatın hayati, siyasi, hukuki, diplomatik sonuçlarından haberdar olamıyorsa,

Yapılan örtülü operasyon başlı başına bir suçsa ve hiçbir yasa, bir suç eylemini meşrulaştırmaya kifayet etmiyorsa,

Bir gazetenin, bir gazetecinin görevi okurunu bilgilendirmek, halkı bu tehlikeden, bu tehditlerden haberdar etmek, bu maceraya kalkışan yetkilileri ikaz etmektir.

Cumhuriyet, bu sorumluluğun bilinciyle bu görüntüleri yayımlıyor.

Cumhuriyet

29 May 2015

Decisions taken, we posed for a photo marking the day and went to work. Everyone knew we were in for a hard night (and many hard days). I went to my office and wrote the leader. Meanwhile, my assistant Ayçin was looking into flights.

Mehmet Ali Birand popped into my mind out of the blue. We had originally met when I was researching for my Master's paper. He was the journalist who had exposed the truth behind the sinking of the *TCG Kocatepe* during the 1974 Cyprus conflict: it had been accidentally sunk by the Turkish Air Force. That scandal was a state secret and writing about it would obviously get the author into trouble. He too had submitted his bombshell a year after the scandal, grabbed his passport and plane ticket and made for the airport.

Forty years later, it was my turn to experience that scene I had described in my paper. I would go to London to visit my son at university there, I decided. All London flights were fully booked, but there was a seat on the Cologne flight.

Just then, I was shown the dummy front page. It looked

stunning. Taking leave of my accomplices, I left the office and went home for the afternoon, surprising and delighting Dilek with my unpredictably early return. The sun was about to set.

'Let's have a glass of wine,' I said, and gave her the news on the terrace as we had some wine and cheese. 'I'm going,' I declared.

'When?'

'Now.'

'Where?'

'To London.'

She understood, though a cloud of anxiety scudded through her eyes at first.

'Will the house be raided?'

'I don't think so, but it's not improbable. Don't stay at home,' I said.

'Perhaps you shouldn't publish?'

I didn't reply.

I was at the Sabiha Gökçen Airport two hours later. My phone rang non-stop. Everyone wanted to know about this bombshell, news of which was spreading like wildfire online. Meanwhile, I received the latest front-page layout on my phone.

I rang Tahir. We discussed what steps we would take in case the print shop was raided. I didn't really like the idea of being away on a night like this, but I had taken a decision – there was no going back. Just then a message arrived which gave me hope that this might be a nice break after all: 'My best mate's coming to London. I'm so happy. The dishes needed doing, dude.'

It was my son Ege. I had yet to see where he'd been living for the past two years, yet to see his college. I was about to meet 'my best mate' – what more could I ask for?

I boarded at 11 p.m. and my mind was on the newspaper and home as we took off. Would the print shop be raided? Would the papers be seized? Would the house be raided in their search for me? I'd been hoping this would be a brief trip; would it turn into a long exile instead?

All this would become clear while I was in the air.

The arrow had left the bow.

I drew on George Orwell's moral support: 'In a time of universal deceit, telling the truth is a revolutionary act.'

2

THREAT

SOME CITIES squander you, others shelter you, and London is the harbour I have sought shelter in goodness knows how many times. As I was rushing there to hide, I recalled my first visit exactly thirty years ago.

At the time I was the Ankara bureau chief of *Nokta*, the bravest magazine of the post-military era. It was run by a great man: Ercan Arıklı. I had his leave to take a journalism course with a six-month bursary, and he was with me on the Ankara–Istanbul leg of my journey.

I remember his whispered 'You're missing a massive bombshell!', then brushing my subsequent enquiries off with an evasive answer. He clearly wanted to keep whatever it was a secret, so I'd pretended to buy it. I was in London by the time I learnt that the bombshell was *Nokta*'s legendary cover story: '*I am a Torturer:* the confessions of a police officer.'

Now, thirty years later, I was going to London with another bombshell in my lap. The city would shelter me once again.

I switched on my mobile the moment we landed in Cologne: all was well. The paper had been printed, not raided! I fell into an anxious and exhausted sleep in a small hotel near the airport. In the morning I was awakened by a hail of telephone calls.

29 May 2015

The exposé had exploded in the already turbulent seas of the election campaign. The state prosecutor had launched an investigation at once and unusually announced it along-side a press release: I would be charged with espionage for having published information that had to remain secret. But who wanted to keep this information secret? I wondered. The MİT? So-called IS? The public? Who would decide?

As Akın said on the phone, 'It's a ridiculous allegation, but what they're trumping up is one that carries a life sentence. It means certain detention. They'd have run you in if it wasn't you. Since they've announced the inquiry, you'll be invited to give a statement. Let's wait a while.'

The serious charge had only intensified the effect of the news. Support calls were raining in.

Leader of the CHP[5] Kılıçdaroğlu said, 'Now we know there are brave journalists in this country. I want you to know I'll always stand by you.'

The centrist media ignored the news. The pro-government media, on the other hand, had gone on the attack. Hatchet men like Cem Küçük[6] indicated the government's stance: 'Should be arrested, but not before the election.'

He and columnist Nagehan Alçı later suggested a more practical solution on a TV programme: 'If this happened in America, say, the *New York Times* published photos of CIA lorries, for example, they'd deal with it without going to the law. The CIA would have taken care of it in a traffic accident.'

I went to London in the middle of this uproar and met

my son. One single hug, and all that gloom vanished. We took a long stroll in Hyde Park and I told him about my years in London without him, and he told me about his in London without me.

The telephone never stopped ringing, dragging me constantly back to the present, back to my country. Weapon-laden lorries kept passing through the magnificent park, piercing the wonderful chat between father and son. One of those calls seared my heart. We'd lost Bedri Koraman, the doyen caricaturist. The least I could do was to go back and attend his funeral. And then I had to give my statement.

It wasn't right that I should stand at a safe distance having thrown down the gauntlet. If there was to be a fight, it had to be joined; if there was a price to pay, I had to be the one to pay it.

I turned a deaf ear to the prompts to 'stay there!' I knew I couldn't stay any longer, and would return. Then something happened on the night of 31 May that validated my decision.

During supper with Ege at Khan's, the famous Indian restaurant, I received a message from Murat Sabuncu:

– *Erdoğan's laying into you on TRT.*

– *What's he saying?*

– *'I've already filed my complaint. They're dying to tarnish Turkey's image. And whoever wrote this special report will pay a heavy price. I'm not letting him get away with it…'*

I read it out to Ege.

2 June 2015   3 June 2015

'How should we respond?' I asked, then tweeted the first thing that popped into my mind: 'The person who committed this crime will pay a heavy price. We're not letting him go that easily...'

The front page of the 2 June edition arrived. The entire editorial staff – with two exceptions – had issued a defiant 'I am responsible'. On the following day, artists rose up, saying, 'We stand by you.' I had to stand by them in turn. I could no longer shelter in the comfort of London in the midst of this storm.

It was time to return after this four-day break. I purchased a ticket on the Istanbul flight with five days left to go before the election.

I copied the entire contents of my laptop onto a hard disk and gave it to Ege for safekeeping. You never knew what they could do if they seized it on my return; they did have form, after all.

That's when I heard that Erdoğan had personally filed a complaint. For the first time ever a President was asking for the heaviest possible punishment for a journalist on a matter that did not appear to be directly connected to him. Such fury could only have emerged from a massive fear. One that could only be concealed under threats, yet revealed itself ever more clearly the harder it was suppressed.

I could smell that fear all the way from London. It was as if I'd written about Erdoğan's personal secrets that had fallen off the back of a lorry, exposed the MİT undersecretary's 'secret transport company' (his 'black box', in his own words).[7]

He had to create a massive dust storm to sweep this under the carpet, just as he had done on 17 December. A dust storm to suffocate opponents like me…

I said goodbye to Ege at the entrance to King's Cross Tube station. It felt like setting off into the unknown. I gave him a hug as I asked, 'What shall I tell your mother?'

'Tell her he's proud of his dad.'

I took wing.

Akın had asked his former colleague Sezgin Tanrıkulu, now a CHP MP, to greet me at the airport in case I was detained there. Lawyers weren't admitted airside, whereas MPs had permanent passes all the way to the immigration desks.

The echoes of the news sank in all the more when I boarded. I made my way through an aisle of cheering as passengers shook my hand and gave me high-fives. The glow of solidarity on their faces wiped away my sense of loneliness. I read about myself in the headlines.

Was I afraid? No. Although it was true we lived 'in the age of fear', the name given to the twentieth century by Albert Camus in a 1946 article for *Combat*.[8] His diagnosis attributed the source of human fear to being bereft of a future. This might not have been the first time we faced fear, but, in the past, words had come to help and had broken down the walls of fear. Yet now, 'No one spoke any longer.' It was this silence that amplified fear. It therefore fell upon us to pierce that isolation, to make a sound, and to challenge fear with words once again. Fear was an empire that feared challenge.

I wasn't afraid. But I was apprehensive.

This apprehension increased as I joined the immigration queue after landing. The police station stood immediately behind the desks; strange how I'd never noticed it before.

I had a small-scale *Midnight Express* moment of tension, worried that my laptop and mobile phone would be seized and used in some kind of set-up. I knew Dilek was waiting at the exit and I wrote her number on a sheet of paper and stuck it on my mobile, planning to hand it to the undergraduate who'd been sitting next to me. I could just ask her to ring this number at the exit and give her the phone.

Then I changed my mind. Transparency... It would be my greatest weapon in this struggle: clarity and transparency against concealed filth. I would draw my strength from transparency.

The officer at the desk looked at my passport first, then at my face... He smiled and stamped the passport. Sezgin Tanrıkulu stood immediately behind the glazed booths. We hugged.

That was the start of a fine month of June.

3

AWARD

AWARDS AND punishments are like the steps of a life ascending to the finale: you proceed by stepping on one, and then the other. One flatters your ego; the next deflates it.

In lands where no success remains unpunished, every cheer is a summons, and yet every trial raises you to new cheering agorae, the day comes when the steps get mixed up: the tyrant's punishment transforms into a shoulder board, whereas the government's award stands out like a banknote stuck on the forehead with spittle.

It is best to proceed on the path you know to be right; neither sitting on your laurels at an award, nor losing heart at a punishment. Awards and punishments will follow come what may.

Which is precisely what happened to me. Throughout 2015,

I was showered first with awards and then with punishments, just like variable weather.

Reeling from the slap delivered by the June ballot box, the government had enough troubles of their own and had to shelve their pledge to bring us to book. Turkey had said 'Halt!' to raving, stifling despotism. Tyranny had been pushed back.

A new June had enkindled a new hope; the public, gagged in the street, had spoken at the ballot box.

That was when *Cumhuriyet* was showered with awards for courageous journalism. Accolades from reputable professional bodies followed one another: the Turkish Publishers' Union and the Turkish Journalists' Society; and then came several international awards, the Dutch PEN being the first to announce the good news.

I was having supper with the pianist Fazıl Say in late summer when my friend Faruk Günaltay rang from Strasbourg to say that Reporters Without Borders had decided to award *Cumhuriyet* the 2015 Press Freedom prize.

What bitter joy. Our newspaper was surrounded by the police.

A suicide bomber captured in Gaziantep was carrying the address and map of the *Cumhuriyet* head office in his pocket. A telephone call from someone at the police headquarters had informed us that the threat was serious, and that we had to evacuate the building. The street was closed to traffic.

The *Cumhuriyet* street closed to traffic, under police tank protection...

That evening we had closed the paper early, and once all our colleagues had left, we had entrusted *Cumhuriyet* to the police tank waiting at the gate, all without panic.

We had left through the police barricade at the entrance to the street in the dark. It looked like a war zone. Friends and family were pressing me to buy a gun, to get a bodyguard or a bulletproof car.

I will never forget our columnist Selçuk Erez dropping in to relate how Ambassador Coşkun Kırca had escaped the ASALA[9] attack in Canada by jumping out to the roof. An anxious Erez cautioned me, 'You must plan where and how to escape in case of a raid...' *Hürriyet*'s head office was mobbed on 6 September, and Ahmet Hakan was attacked on 1 October. The assailants had been protected by both the police and the judiciary, and later even rewarded by the ruling party.

Cumhuriyet was targeted both by the government and by so-called IS.

A storm braved in the name of journalism, so we could breach the silence of the capitulated media. That was the environment in which I wrote my speech for the Reporters Without Borders award ceremony in Strasbourg:

'Our building is surrounded by the police and my office has two windows. One gives on to the courthouse, and the other to a cemetery. These are the two places Turkish journalists visit most frequently…'

Silivri had yet to come into my sights.

* * *

Turkey was on fire. A horror film had been rushed onto the screens in a matter of five months as suicide bomber massacres flooded city squares with blood. White Renault Toroses, the nightmare of the '90s, were back on stage.

In the snare of every ogre imaginable, a blunt knife pressing at the throat of society prodded, 'Vote, and this will stop.' Cowed masses were in no state to grasp that voting for the knife would only invite it to plunge deeper.

A bleeding nation was on its knees.

And fell for it.

The ruling party polled 5 million new votes in the 1 November general election. This was the triumph of fear.

Camus's diagnosis had come and struck Turkey seventy years later: masses despairing of a future had been afraid and sought shelter under the seemingly most powerful wings. But it was those wings they had to fear most…

Because the holder of the knife and the unfolder of the wing were one and the same. We fell into the trap.

Sunday 1 November was the night of a political earthquake. The return of the nightmare…

Voters who had forced servitude into a five-month break had changed their minds, like helpless, battered wives with nowhere else to go returning to more beatings at the marital home. A far stronger wave of oppression awaited us now.

Faces began dropping as the early results came in. No one said a word. It was as if we had lost the fortress we'd conquered earlier. We were weary and unarmed.

That night, Ege rang from London. He was glued to the screen: 'It's heartbreaking to watch our homeland slip away like this,' he said.

He had spent fourteen years out of his twenty – meaning he had grown up – under Erdoğan; yet this could have been the beginning. Tahir whispered in some corner as we were

preparing the front page, 'I think you should leave tonight.'
He meant out of the country.

'They'll come and get you in the morning, and you'll waste
four years banged up.' As if there had been a coup. It was
like the night of 12 September, and those – like Tahir – who
had been banged up, who'd tasted prison, knew all too well
about the difficulty of going to prison in this stage of our lives.
All too aware that our phones were tapped, my mother offered a dismal 'You know I'd never ask why if anyone wanted to
live elsewhere...'

I got home in the early hours. Dilek was unhappy too.

'Perhaps you ought to go,' she said.

For many years I had heard tales of exile, and had even
covered some in documentaries. Most had been unhappy;
homesickness had debilitated some and even killed a few.
Besides, I had a fair idea of what lay in store. I expected it.
I would chance it. I would stay, and continue to tell the truth
even if I were to be imprisoned.

The newspaper management meeting following the election resolved to maintain our present upright stance. That the
media would do an about face was obvious; there was even a
greater need for *Cumhuriyet* now. Hope was the only antidote
to fear, and we would be its spokespeople. We wouldn't stand
by and watch as the land where our children were born and
raised was taken from us.

The ventriloquist spoke through Cem Küçük immediately after the election.

'I've spoken with the top authority,' Küçük declared. 'The treachery of the MİT lorries will never be forgiven.'

It was something Erdoğan had said personally months ago anyway, except the delay meant the legal complaint period had expired. But who cared? The entire state mechanism was now in hand.

Unwinding with a glass of something on Friday after work had become a recent office ritual. On one of those occasions, our veteran crime reporter Canan Coşkun blurted out, 'Be aware: if they call you up for a statement, you'll be arrested,' as she related her impressions at the Çağlayan Justice Palace. I suspect that was the day when the issue of detention first popped into my mind.

I was amongst the journalists the CHP leader Kılıçdaroğlu met on 5 November 2015. Interpreting Cem Küçük's words as 'proof that we're now in the Goebbels regime', he added, 'Who's spurring him on?'

We all knew the answer.

Sadly, that meeting also exposed that very few of us could defy Goebbels. Kılıçdaroğlu's reference to Nazism didn't make it into any of the newspapers represented at that meeting – except for *Cumhuriyet*, of course.

The centre could not hold. Now it was time to run in those opposing it, haul them into the 'centre'.

On 8 November, Hamdi Gezmiş[10] and I went to Essen for Literatürk Festival. The readers packed into the city library all asked the same questions:

'What's going to happen now?'

'Aren't you scared for your life?'

'Are you going to continue to write your acerbic columns?'

I replied, 'There is a price to pay if you're a journalist or a writer in Turkey. Unless you're prepared to pay it, you should never pick up the pen in the first place…'

Semra Uzun-Önder, one of the organisers, was amongst those concerned. On Sunday morning, she took me for a sunny stroll along a peaceful waterway.

'I know you. You can't cope inside. You'd fester. Take your family and come here. Write your columns and books. Criticise freely to your heart's content here.'

Freely… How wonderful the sound of that word under a smiling sun – possibly for the last time on the eve of a charmless winter! I was walking freely at a calm spot for the first time after months of turmoil. Peace on this bank, although what lay on the other could have been an abominable swamp.

The guardians of darkness waited to bury me in mud. The moment I crossed the bridge, the sun would vanish behind a cloud, a battle to the death would start and a heavy iron door would quite probably shut behind me. For goodness knew how many years…

This bank looked open, free and bright. A man with a cause fought on the other bank as a harmless writer walked here. Gemini, my ruling sign, was hesitating once again: one foot on one bank, and the other on the opposite: to dedicate myself to the book shaping in my mind away from this dirty fight, the filth of a muddy pool and the growing regime of oppression, and to maintain that freedom I breathed in during that sunny stroll on that Sunday.

It was possible. Close enough to become reality if I were to decide there and then...

I realised I had reached a crossroads at the end of that long walk. One path led to captivity, the other to freedom... One to courage, the other to exile.

HERKES İÇİN SINAV DÖNEMİ

CUMHURİYET'E, onun aydınlanmacı mücadelesine, kararlı direncine en çok şimdi ihtiyaç var. » CAN DÜNDAR 3'te

9 November 2015

I returned to the hotel, powered up my laptop and began tapping on the keys for my regular Monday editorial. My fingers hit the stiff keys uncontrollably, as if composing a declaration of war.

The lines that poured forth spoke of *Cumhuriyet*'s resolve not to give in to hatchet men's empty threats, to continue to fight alone if need be for its principles as it had done up to now, and to speak out with the courage befitting its history in this time of great silence.

I sent it off to the paper. I felt better.

The twins scrapping within had stopped; the peace-seeking side tugging at my jacket, 'Stay here, write your book,' had lost.

I would follow the other, the one who had chosen to fight.

* * *

Akın and I travelled to Strasbourg on 17 November to pick up the prize awarded to *Cumhuriyet* by Reporters Without Borders. Our wives Dilek and Adalet came along. It was a wonderful ceremony and I felt as if the world was holding our hands. But the world wasn't in a better state either.

Cathedral Square was watched over by patrols carrying heavy weaponry since the attacks by so-called IS in Paris.

With Akın Atalay at the award ceremony in Strasbourg

Fear, the sickness of our age, had captured the elderly continent.

The next morning, as we were having coffee, the Secretary General of Reporters Without Borders Christophe Deloire made an anxious admission, 'We're worried about you.' He then added that they could help if I wished to stay in France.

We had only just met. But with years of supporting journalists who gave everything in their struggle with oppressive regimes, he knew what lay in store.

So did I. Except I just couldn't accept running like a criminal instead of the real criminals, or end up being in the wrong when I was right. They had to see that they couldn't intimidate everyone. I chose imprisonment in Turkey to freedom in exile.

Christophe gave me a friendly handshake as we parted and said, 'Rest assured; we'll always stand beside you.' Which he did.

As we boarded our flight back, all four of us were aware we were travelling towards a prison.

We held our award.

Now it was time for the punishment.

4

PUNISHMENT

'SOMEONE MUST have been telling lies about Josef K., for one morning, without having done anything wrong, he was arrested.'

That's how Kafka starts *The Trial*. K. was the first person to pop into my mind that morning.

I found a note on the desk when I arrived at my office.

Deputy Chief Prosecutor İrfan Fidan has summoned you to give a statement at 11.00 on Thursday 26 November.

It was Tuesday 24 November. Erdoğan had approved the Third Davutoğlu Cabinet, Turkey's sixty-fourth. And the freshly endorsed Premier had stated, 'Freedom of the press is our red line.' His first act was to pass red. The summons on my desk was the first act of the new government. Such was their impatience.

This was, in effect, the news we'd been anticipating for months … But they were too late. In the midst of all that chaos – elections, coalition negotiations etc. – they had missed the four-month deadline; the statute of limitations would now apply. That was the reason for the government's hurry.

I dropped in on my neighbour Akın to ask, 'What do you think?' He laughed. 'They've missed the train,' he said. It had already been 180 days since the image was published: the four-month filing period had lapsed. As a lawyer, he suffered under the delusion that you could still trust the law.

'Arresting you wouldn't be like arresting anyone else, anyway. It would cause an uproar both in the country and abroad,' he added.

That I had been invited by a telephone call was another encouraging point. If there had been an ulterior motive, I would have been taken away from home in an early-morning raid. But then why was I summoned for a date two days hence instead?

Perhaps they'd hoped I might leave the country in the interim. My phone was tapped; the recommendations of friends and family could not have been a secret. If I were to be caught trying to leave the country in this period, I'd have looked guilty from the off. If they were to turn a blind eye to my flight, they'd be rid of me.

But my mind was made up. I would transform this trial into

a counteraction, use it as the foundation to expose the truth and bring the real criminals to justice.

That was the morning of the Russian fighter jet incident: an SU24 had been downed on the Syrian border. The government had started off with a crisis. This was the first clue to the unstable 'New Turkey'. That same day, referring to the weapons in the MİT lorry, Erdoğan let slip, 'So there were weapons; so what?' A clear admission – he had just verified the news item. He had grown brazen enough to exclaim, 'Weapons, schmeapons!'

Of course: he was in power. Who could hold him to account? 'Fine; and ours was news, so what?'

The real surprise was that our Ankara Bureau Chief Erdem Gül was also summoned; it was he who had published the gendarme inventory of the weapons, the report that had dispelled all possible doubt. So he would be made to pay too.

We convened in the big meeting room on *Cumhuriyet*'s fifth floor at 3.45 p.m. The same team as on 28 May, except Erdem was also present this time, looking quite relaxed.

I pre-empted the lawyers: 'You're all thinking, "We told you so," right?'

They were. But they were all stunned by the gravity of the charges too: *Obtaining and disclosing confidential state documents with the purpose of political or military espionage* and *aiding and abetting an armed terrorist organisation.*

I couldn't stop myself laughing: 'Espionage?' and recalled that lovely prayer of Demirel's: 'God save you from an apposite slur.'

This was pretty inapposite. Who would believe us to be spies? And Gülenists even?[11] Weren't we their greatest critics when the government and the congregation were hand in glove? Wasn't it the *Cumhuriyet* that had been hurt most by them both?

Wasn't it Erdoğan who had actually aided and abetted the congregation? Wasn't it he who lamented, 'Haven't we given them everything they asked for?' Just because they had fallen out, could he live down that former complicity and accuse us instead?

The answer was, 'You can't put anything past him.'

'In that case,' I replied, 'My defence is already prepared. I'd written my Master's paper on state secrets; this is my forte. I'll have a 200-page defence drawn up by tomorrow.'

Then we went into detail. We'd be quizzed about our source, which we had the right not to divulge. But it might help to deny any connection with the congregation. I had a better idea: if I were really pushed, I would state 'the footage was posted on a flash drive' and confess 'to having suspected it had been sent by Hakan Fidan, the Undersecretary of MİT'.

Naturally no undersecretary would want his agency to be implicated in a crime, after all… Perhaps that was his way of warning the public. My tactics of fooling İrfan Fidan with Hakan Fidan only raised a bitter smile amongst the lawyers.

'Then give me the best- and worst-case scenarios,' I said.

The best case was I would be released on bail, i.e. with a ban on foreign travel. But given the seriousness of the charge, and the fact that the decision lay solely with the criminal courts that were under total government control, this probability was quite remote.

Akın said, 'The risk of detention is quite high.'

'How long would we be banged up for?' I asked.

'Three years,' guessed Bülent Utku.

Akın and Tora Pekin said, 'One year.'

Bülent and Abbas were of the opinion we shouldn't go to prison.

Akın said, 'I'd have stayed.'

Tora summed up, 'You'll probably go down.'

Tahir offered his caveat: 'They should go away. The rule of law's gone. No one who goes in comes out.'

That was also true.

It was impossible for us to be convicted for revealing an 'open secret'; on the other hand, they could intervene with false documents and information as they'd learnt from the Gülenists,[12] fling us into a much bigger congregation case, delay the indictment and thus punish us with a long pre-trial detention well ahead of a verdict.

It would be helpful to appear before a regular judge first, and even get a conviction and appeal to the Constitutional Court and even the European Court of Human Rights.

My mind was still on Josef K. as we debated all this. He also looks for a way of getting a guilty verdict as soon as possible to escape the clutches of a judiciary system moving at a snail's pace – his only hope as he sees it.

Ahmet Cemal's foreword in *The Trial* could have been written with us in mind:

When the prevention of conviction is synonymous with the prevention of acquittal, the accused have no other course than to get themselves convicted to be free.

We could have been going for a hearing in *The Trial* by Kafka…

Erdem and I agreed: we would go and offer our statements, come what may.

We were in a routine news meeting as *#CumhuriyetSummoned* spread across social media. Not, I must add, a particularly unusual occurrence, given we were summoned several times every week…

I emerged from the news meeting and went straight into the advertising meeting with Ayşe Cemal. As she waxed lyrical about projects that would take the newspaper out of its present dire straits, my mind was on the defence I'd make the following day. I wasn't paying attention; it was best to open up. I interrupted her: 'I'm going to jail tomorrow, Ayşe,' slipped out.

It sounded strange even to me.

Ayşe was shocked. She paused, paled, and ended the meeting saying, 'Oh God… Oh God…'

That evening, after finishing at the paper, a large crowd of us strolled over to the Hamdi Restaurant. We had a great time and enjoyed several drinks while prison veterans gave advice and told old lag tales.

Farewell supper at the Hamdi Restaurant

Önder Çelik[13] and I had been wracking our brains for months to raise circulation; the temptation to tease him proved too strong to resist: 'Print a much higher run on the day after;

if *this* doesn't increase your circulation, I don't know what will!'

It was as though I was about to carry out a regular requirement of the job, as though I was going to get treatment for an occupational hazard.

Erdem and I raised our glasses to all our friends at that table. That would be the last drop of rakı we would have for a long time…

That night at home, I chose the books I would want in prison. I would finally have the time to write the book I'd been planning for quite a while. Dilek and I avoided discussing this too much, although we both knew hard times awaited. Except we believed we would overcome; this, too, would pass, and it wouldn't be the first time.

The following day was 26 November. We would be celebrating our twenty-eighth wedding anniversary.

5

COURT

MY LATE grandmother always started with a kindly, 'Oh,' and 'God is great, son,' no matter what the topic was, no matter how important or trivial. Her unshakeable belief would make you assume that no evil deed would ever be left unpunished and that no injustice would prevail upon the earth.

'God is great!' consoles the victim and threatens revenge upon the vain.

Whenever grandmother tucked the end between the headscarf and her right cheek and said, 'God is great' I would believe that the kid who'd stolen my marbles would return them all and then turn to stone.

In time, when the marbles refused to return, the thieves were rewarded – never mind punished – and it was the dispossessed who turned to stone, I began to launch into questions: 'If he's that great, why doesn't he break thieving hands? Why doesn't he return my marbles? Why does he withhold his mercy?'

Whenever I asked these questions, she would shush me with a 'Repent!' and shelter in the only justice she trusted: 'God is great!'

I rang my mother on the morning of Thursday 26 November, before going to the courthouse to explain the situation. She said, 'God is great, son,' on the phone, as if tucking into my inner pocket an amulet handed down from one generation to the next.

We still stood on the side expecting divine justice, but the marble nicking business was in the hands of others who constantly took His name.

We were on our way to stand to account before those we should be holding to account. Thankfully, 'God was great.'

It was rainy.

I had no idea whether I'd be tucking into a celebratory dinner or an inmate's rations that evening. All the same, I wore my smartest velvet jacket and my favourite shirt with the concealed button placket. Suitable for defence as well as celebration. I gazed at the leaden sea for quite a while before leaving the house, and then hugged Cinnamon. I might be able to see everyone else if I were to be banged up, but not my dog.

Which is precisely what happened.

Cinnamon sending me off at the door

The Justice Palace was surrounded by friendly faces: writers, journalists, MPs, and my comrades at *Cumhuriyet* had all hurried over. Some I'd stood by on their rainy day were now standing by me on mine, voluntary lawyers all.

There were so many, although most didn't believe we'd be arrested. We were summoned so frequently that few thought it would be different this time. I gave a short statement at the door:

'We're not spies, traitors or heroes; we're simply journalists. We're here to defend journalism and the public's right to

be informed. This time they're not facing a newspaper or journalists ready to be cowed. This time they're facing journalists
who are determined to follow this matter up, who will stand
upright and defend their words.'

It was strange for a journalist who had spent years inter-
viewing behind the camera to be now interviewed *facing* the
camera; but this was not my choice.

I had once been invited for a chat at the Justice Palace, a
place where I had given statement after statement. The then
newly appointed Chief Prosecutor Hadi Salihoğlu had invited
me for a cup of tea to complain about a news item. We'd had a
long chat. He had moaned about Gülenists, saying, 'They've
bugged you too.'

It was perplexing that such an obvious piece of information
was mentioned in passing. I remember leaving with a pen-
knife in my pocket, his memento – apparently customary in
his part of the world. I now entered through the door with a
pen in my pocket, the door through which I'd left with a pen-
knife on that day.

As I walked through that door, the government's hatchet
men announced on pro-government TV stations: 'He'll be
arrested today,' as I was to learn later.

We stepped into the prosecutor's office at 11.20 a.m.

İrfan Fidan's courteous greeting was faultless and he

maintained the same cheerful courtesy throughout the statements. He explained that the MİT Undersecretary Hakan Fidan was no relation. Tora and I sat on the black leather sofa facing his desk. Akın Atalay and Bülent Utku took the armchairs facing each other. A clerk was sitting at a small desk to the right of the prosecutor.

As we sipped our teas, the prosecutor pointed to the thick blue folders on the document cabinet. This was the 10,000-page file on the Selam Tevhid investigation. The prosecutor had alleged that the Gülenist Terror Organisation (FETÖ, from Fethullah, the cleric's forename) had attempted to overthrow the government, ostensibly alleging a probe into a terrorist organisation called the Palestine Army. The objective – as far as I could make out – was to arrest the Undersecretary of MİT, prevent a thaw in Turkish–Iranian relations and scupper the peace process. To this end, they'd wiretapped hundreds of people. There were 2,280 tapes, most recordings concerning private lives.

'Is this allowed in the *Risale*?'[14] asked the prosecutor, referring to the Gülenists: how could they justify their actions?

We were curious to see how he'd bring the subject round to us. What did all this have to do with us? No one knew for certain if we hadn't been bugged too! Why treat us as suspects in an investigation when we should have been the plaintiffs?

It seems we had aided and abetted the FETÖ 'unwittingly'.

We had 'divulged state secrets'. So the 'secret' was true: that is, the lorries *were* carrying weapons. And this had to 'remain a secret'.

'Yes,' said the prosecutor. 'Those weapons were intended for the Turkmens of Aleppo.'

'You might like to question the Deputy Prime Minister Tuğrul Türkeş,' I said. As everyone knew, before crossing the floor and settling into his new chair, Türkeş had issued an unequivocal denial, 'I swear those weapons were *not* going to the Turkmens.' And this is where the theoretical aspect of the matter came into play.

Who had the right to decide what could be known, and what could not? The government of the day, of course. Well, what if the government were committing a crime? What if that crime was concealed under the stamp of 'secret'? Who would monitor that?

In the USA, the press occasionally undertook this mission. The American press had exposed so many scandals: the ruling party bugging the opposition's headquarters, the army's crimes in Vietnam, and shipment of weapons to Iran breaching the embargo. All these scandals had led to the prosecution of the guilty authorities... not of the journalists who had revealed them.

In our case, MİT was undertaking a mission it was not legally empowered to do and, by supplying weapons for a neighbouring country's civil war, was committing a crime. A crime that might have been in the government's interest to conceal, and a journalist's duty to expose. This is what distinguished a journalist from a civil servant.

The prosecutor asked, 'Can an intelligence agency admit it's shipping weapons?'

'Of course not,' I replied. 'But neither could any journalist ignore an intelligence agency that is shipping weapons illegally.'

Perhaps because he had restricted his reading to civil servant-minded journalists, the prosecutor was struggling to appreciate an attitude that disregards 'the state's interest'. Yet, what was hailed as the 'state's interest' was all too frequently nothing more than the interest of the government at the time. It fell upon us to defend the 'public interest' against this trap.

'So you think anything could be news then?'

His curiosity was quite genuine. He even offered a peculiar example to illustrate his point: 'You do know about the German Chancellor's naked photos taken when she was very young. The German papers didn't publish them. Would you publish my naked photo if you found it? Are there no limits?'

'Public interest defines the limits,' I replied. 'There's absolutely no public benefit to publishing naked photos of politicians, neither Merkel's nor yours. But if the state is caught out with its pants down in an illicit affair, I wouldn't hesitate for a moment to publish them.'

I then explained why publishing this news was in the public interest:

'The relationship network exposed by Susurluk[15] was also a state secret. It was only through that accident that the state's criminal complicity with murderers came to light. Just as well, too; at least some of that was cleaned out. Ergenekon was a state secret. By choosing to eliminate the opposition, the government squandered the opportunity to solve it. What if the state is committing crimes today? What if those weapons end up in the wrong hands, say, ISIL's, for instance? What if Turkey was dragged into the quagmire that is Syria, into a war, without Parliament's knowledge? Who's going to check it? Who's going to warn the public? Don't Parliament and the public have a right to know? Perhaps that report even assisted the state by preventing a grave mistake.'

Several cups of tea later, the prosecutor still didn't look convinced. He believed the interception of the MİT lorries was a trap set for the Republic of Turkey. And it was Fethullah Gülen who had sprung the trap.

'And we belong to that organisation, do we?' I asked.

'We'd be laughed out of court if we claimed you were,' said the prosecutor.

I couldn't resist it: 'Mr Prosecutor; this peril you've only just noticed is one I and my newspaper have been fighting against for years. Besides, when we asked, "Are you aware of the danger?", the entire apparatus of the state stood together with the congregation to confront us. And now here you are, the state at your back, telling us about the peril posed by the congregation. If there's anyone you have to interrogate here, it's those who'd been lamenting, "Haven't we given them everything they asked for?" Could there be a better admission of aiding and abetting?'

I then reminded him of our interrogation by the prosecutor of that congregation; the once powerful prosecutor Zekeriya Öz was now a fugitive abroad.[16] Revenge was a dish consumed well before it was allowed to cool in Turkey. Just then, Akın cited a great example:

'When the party in power and the Gülenists were in partnership, we had published an encrypted Ministry of Foreign Affairs message. The Foreign Secretary was instructing Turkish embassies to support the congregation's schools abroad. We were tried at the time for exposing activities aiding and abetting the congregation.'

In other words, our stance on the congregation hadn't changed one iota – it was the government's that had.

They had come to our viewpoint, but were trying to live down their previous partnership by attacking us. For my part, I was waiting for the prosecutor to present his evidence, wondering how the allegation of abetting the congregation would be substantiated. He asked four questions, one after the other:

'Is this your telephone number?' – 'Yes.'

'Did it belong to you between such and such dates?' – 'Yes.'

'X person and Y person had exchanged messages the night before the report was published, saying, "The footage is going to be published." Are you aware of this exchange?' – 'No.'

'Do you know these people?' –'No.'

That was all.

Really?

Where were the bugged tapes revealing FETÖ instructing us? Faked telephone conversations – 'Publish such-and-such and your money's ready'? Bank accounts or scandalous photos of clandestine meetings?

Nowhere to be seen. There was nothing. Not a single thing.

It seemed that the state's fake document production capacity had taken a serious knock after the falling out with the Gülenists. Would they arrest us on an allegation of espionage based on a Twitter exchange between two people we didn't know? We emerged smiling from the two-hour interview…

'It doesn't look like much,' I said to the friends waiting in anticipation at the door. I must confess, I couldn't predict an arrest after such an insubstantial interrogation.

Nevertheless, accustomed to the 'good cop/bad cop' game, my lawyers favoured prudence. We sat down on the floor with our friends waiting in the hallways and lunched on toasted sandwiches and Ayran, Kemal Türkler's daughter Nilgün's treat.

The clerk emerged presently and announced the prosecutor's order: 'To court for arrest…'

A cloud of bewilderment scudded through the hallways, and then it rained rage. How could two journalists be arrested on such a grave charge – 'political–military espionage' – for a couple of news reports published in the paper?

My telephone was ringing non-stop. Kemal Kılıçdaroğlu railed, 'Reporting is a crime in 21st-century Turkey!' as Selahattin Demirtaş thundered, 'This is the worst kind of abomination!'

An incredulous Sezen Aksu was crying. Celalettin Can and Mahmut Tanal were offering tips on how to pace in the yard.[17]

The Şişli Constabulary officers had settled into a corner, ready to take their charges. And we expected justice from a criminal court under total government control. I wondered what was taking place in the background.

As I gazed around me, I could have been shooting my own documentary.

My colleagues, who'd been kept out of the hallway, were arguing with the private security officers beyond the police barrier. Hearing Murat Sabuncu's stentorian tones, I texted him: 'Don't argue, OK?'

Aslı Aydıntaşbaş warned users, retweeting #CanDundar IsntAlone, 'Can Dündar is utterly alone. We're at the courthouse, and there's no one here other than a few MPs and friends. Shame.'

The leader of the ÖDP, Alper Taş, was using his mobile phone to broadcast on Periscope. Can Öz was amongst the Can Publishing crew anxiously waiting for the outcome. Dilek and I could have been hosting a 'justice party': we chatted to each and every one of our guests as we commented on the prosecutor's decision.

We were summoned into the criminal court at 5.45 p.m.

Waiting for the ruling... Photo: Enis Berberoğlu

One glance at the judge, and I knew what to expect...

He looked us up and down like a doctor about to pro-nounce, 'Eat what you like now,' or proclaim, 'This is the court order; say what you like now.' Our defence given earlier to the prosecutor was repeated and recorded under the judge's apathetic gaze.

The pro-government tweeter *Secret Archive* had already announced our arrest at 8.04 p.m., and so by this time we had been waiting eleven hours for a court order that had already been given.

I composed a tweet – *We are arrested* – but wouldn't press *send* until the moment the order was announced.

We were summoned back into the chamber before long. It was now 9.20 p.m. The judge spoke with the same rancorous expression for about ten seconds and announced our arrest before hightailing it. I heard a yell from somewhere behind: 'Shame on you!'

I turned towards the door and called out, 'Arrest order, guys!' In a journalistic instinct, I'd announced my own news. I pressed the send button on the tweet: *We are arrested.*

The courtroom was in uproar. Friends shook my hand. Someone tucked a ringing mobile into my palm; it was Kılıç-daroğlu: 'Too harsh!' he said. 'Stand firm; we'll always be with you.'

I then exchanged a few sentences with Demirtaş, who also spoke encouragingly. That's when the plainclothesmen entered the courtroom and said we had to go. I handed Akın my notebook (my constant companion) and mobile phone.

Just then, Halk TV connected to a live broadcast. All I could say was, 'Don't worry. This is like a badge of honour for us. Inside or out makes no difference under such a government. We will continue the struggle, inside or out.'

I embraced Dilek and whispered, 'Happy anniversary.'

I waved at the courtroom as friends chanted, 'Can't stifle the free press!'

And we were going to the place where the free press was stifled: to Silivri.

6

ROAD

I'LL NEVER forget İsmet Pasha's maxim: 'I embark upon each new era as if starting a new life.'

A lesson in resistance distilled from life…

The victorious commander had swapped soldier's boots for patent leathers, became Foreign Secretary and later Prime Minister. Later still, after falling out with President Mustafa Kemal, he retreated into a self-induced solitude, before eventually ascending to the presidency. He was ousted again later, then in opposition, then in power…

Life takes you to the pinnacle before dropping you into the abyss, like the big dipper in a fairground. Fortune alternately smiles and frowns; the secret to coping with its vagaries is the realisation that neither the pinnacles nor the abysses are permanent.

So long as you can remember the abyss when you're at the top, and the pinnacle when you're at the bottom, neither the abyss will seem so wretched, nor the pinnacle so splendid. They're both part of life.

As I walked out of the courtroom door, I knew I was entering a new era in my life – I was walking from freedom into captivity. At that point, however, it was too early to decide whether it would lead to a pinnacle or to an abyss. Only time would tell.

The door opened to a long hallway. The police officer beside me asked if I needed anything.

'Justice,' I replied.

He'd meant the toilet.

'No need,' I smiled.

Six or seven anti-terror squad officers escorted me down to the car park. Erdem was also brought down. We were like the reluctant actors in a tedious play.

'You must be hungry,' said the bearded officer with long hair.

We were. He sent one of his colleagues off to buy some biscuits and courteously offered Erdem a cigarette. Spotting our solicitors Akın and Bülent was like a breath of fresh air.

'We'll see each other much more frequently now,' said Akın.

He rang Dilek and asked her to pack my things, then we said our goodbyes.

We set off, three officers – one at the wheel – and us. They didn't press my head down as we got into the car like I'd always seen on news bulletins, flank me on the rear seat or handcuff me. We set off as if going for a spin – down the road I took daily on my way to the newspaper, the road I always willed to end. This time I was willing it not to. Patiently...

'Welcome, patience,' I said to myself, greeting this old friend I'd been neglecting for quite a while: 'We're together for a while now. Hurry can take a break now...'

Familiar buildings, shops, pavements and people all swept past the car windows in ones and twos. They all looked different that night. I was trying to carve their images into my mind, not something I'd ever felt the need to do before.

Our first stop was the Eyüp State Hospital for a medical check-up. Accident and Emergency was teeming with weary, pallid and resigned patients. I entered, avoiding their gaze. I was neither sick, nor a criminal, yet here I was: brought amongst the sick, dressed as a criminal. I didn't want to be seen in that state.

The officers didn't grab my arms, but they were alert all the same. We entered a small room next to the emergency entrance, whereupon an astonished young doctor stared at me.

'Wish I had my mobile here!' he exclaimed.

A snapshot could have been the souvenir of this unexpected encounter.

'Any battery?' he asked.

'No,' I replied.

'Fine, let's not keep you then,' he said.

My medical was done in one minute. We set off again. I wondered what was happening behind us. Was Turkey asleep? Or had it awakened from that deep slumber?

'Where now?' I asked the officer sitting next to me.

'To Silivri,' he replied. 'It's quite a way. Best take a bit of a rest now...'

He'd noticed my exhaustion. I tried to doze off; to no avail. I could feel the distance between freedom and me growing on this journey into captivity. As if captivity would last as long as the journey itself...

The silence in the car was broken by the voice of the officer sitting next to me.

'I'd read one of your columns, about Atatürk and the Education Secretary...'

What a surprise. An old column had fetched up from the archives and melted the iceberg between this officer and me. I launched into an account of Reşit Galip.

A young, audacious and radical educator, he was courageous enough to defy Atatürk even at the latter's table, an act that Atatürk had rewarded with a Cabinet post. *Our Oath*, repeated at the start of every school day, was his work.

It was a snippet of history that fascinated my escort on our way to Silivri. The conversation then moved to the downed Russian fighter jet and the potential ramifications of the incident. I was nibbling the biscuits in the pocket behind the front seat in the meantime.

I'd been dreaming of an elegant anniversary dinner with Dilek somewhere nice, and here I was, gnawing at biscuits in a police car on the way to Silivri. Reverie: silverware; reality: Silivri…

We stopped briefly at the Selimpaşa services with some 15km to go. As he smoked, Erdem, trying to strike up a conversation, asked our escort how realistic TV police dramas were.

'Not that realistic,' they replied, mentioning a few inconsistencies they'd spotted.

Just then, another vehicle parked next to us and a young couple descended. Spotting me, they wanted to come over; when the officers intervened, the young couple called out, 'We're with you!'

Ammunition for the soul popping up in the middle of the night, in the middle of nothingness. A message that tells us we're not alone. The first light in the darkness.

We were near Silivri.

I wondered how my mother was. Ege? Dilek's parents? My loved ones? Those who loved me? My friends?

'I wish they knew I was having fun, albeit secretly; I wish I could tell them not to worry,' I thought to myself.

It was the toughest time for the paper from a financial point of view; we were on the verge of some difficult decisions. The mortgage repayments were crippling. And there I was, wishing I could take the phone off the hook and lose myself in a new book – which is precisely what happened, to the extent that I was planning the introduction as Silivri appeared on the horizon.

The twelve-hour Justice Palace adventure came to an end 80km later, at the Silivri gates.

The sign above the massive gate read: 'The Silivri Penitentiaries Campus'. I wondered what penalty we would serve, given we had not been sentenced in the first place? And 'campus' always meant a university to me. But it was different this time.

Goodbye to freedom at the Silivri gate

Journalists were camped at the gate. I was reminded of the paparazzi shows where the celebrity is spotted. 'Spotted with a plainclothes man at the Silivri gates' flashed through my mind as an amusing imaginary headline.

I wished I could get out of the car to explain to my fellow journalists that this struggle was also about their prospects of doing their job under far freer conditions. Tell them that so long as this lawless brutality, this arrogant tyranny continued, soon they would be utterly unable to write anything, soon they would all be cloaked in silence. Warn them that anyone insisting on reporting the news and rebelling against censorship would end up in that same prison at whose gates they now stood. Something, to be fair, most knew anyway...

So many that had gone through that gate before us had spoken out and proved it.

Silivri's foundations had been laid three years after Erdoğan had come to power. It opened in 2008 and soon became a concentration camp for his opponents.

We, the latest guests of the camp, crossed beyond the great wall near midnight. The soil ended and a heap of concrete began, stretching like the Great Wall of China. There were walls and barbed wire everywhere. This was a land of concrete and iron... Slaveland... With watchtowers and charmless, single-storey buildings connected by spotlighted narrow lanes leading to deserted stone courtyards painted dirty yellow.

We stopped at the last courtyard and descended from the car. A vast iron door opened. We stepped in. Life stayed outside.

The officers handed us over to the warders, now called 'penitentiary protection officers'. Navy-blue uniforms led us from a wide doorway sporting a forest of cameras in the corners into a reception room. There were two computers on two desks to book us in; except, the programme just wouldn't start up. We were eventually admitted after a series of tedious questions and a long and enervating wait: mother's name, father's name, address, telephone number, eye and hair colour…

Exhausted as we were, we still giggled trying to recall bald Erdem's hair colour.

Our personal effects were taken away for secure storage – cards, money, photographs, watches, pens – whatever we had. Then fingertips and palms were pressed onto an inkpad and our prints were taken. Ink, the blood of our pens for all these years, was now recording our details. And finally it was time for the photos.

We were asked to stand in front of a wall.

'Our pictures were took on a blank page.'[18]

We were now registered detainees.

At this point it was well past midnight. By the time the registration process had been completed, we could barely stand up. I was taken in before Erdem, through a moving walkway and an electronic search gate like those found at airports. I began walking down a Silivri corridor, escorted by a warder in front and one at the rear. Iron grille doors opened, closed; new corridors led us to new barred doors. At the end of a long corridor, we turned into a narrower one.

This was A1 street – our street… There were eight cells in the corridor. We stopped before the fifth door. This was my new address.

'We have to search you,' they said.

I extended exhausted arms out to the sides and opened my legs. A warder patted me down all the way from the neck down to the trouser hems, and then scanned my body with a security wand. And finally it was the turn of the shoes. 'The shoes,' he said.

This was the first in what would be a ritual repeated hundreds of times during my time inside Silivri. I removed the left shoe first. He took it, tipped it over and tapped it on the floor. Then the process was repeated with the right. It, too, was 'clean'.

Once the search was done, the other warder unlocked the brown iron door. Three locks in all: first the key, then the bolt, and finally the screw iron handle.

The iron door closed behind my back with a 'God save you.'

That's how I entered my new bachelor pad.

7

NIGHT

I LEFT the 'Justice Palace' and entered the 'Injustice Palace', that jail so easy to enter and yet so hard to leave. It was like stepping into a time machine…

Can you go back a century in one step? I did. That night. In a cell in Silivri. There were none of the objects that had entered our lives in the last century, like mobile phones, computers or the internet.

22 February 2016, *Bugün*

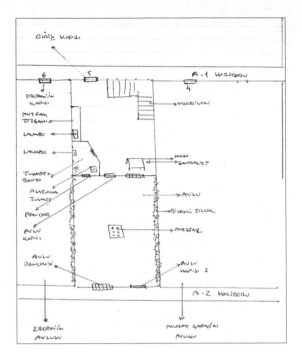

Can Dündar's sketch of the 'villa's ground floor

No social media, Facebook or Twitter, no washing machine, dishwasher or fridge, no TV, radio or table lamp. Not even a rug, curtain, armchair or teapot. Nothing. A minimalist style had been attempted here.

It's probably easier to write what *was* there: a white plastic table; white plastic chair; three iron beds; three metal wardrobes; one kitchen worktop; and a steel cupboard.

That's all.

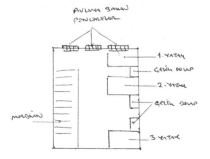

Can Dündar's sketch of the 'villa's first floor

The room and I stared at each other. My black velvet jacket looked the white plastic chair up and down, as if to say, 'I must have come to the wrong wedding.'

I stared at the cell like a flat-seeker unmoved by the offering of a pushy estate agent. It wasn't that small at all. A two-storey villa of 25 sq. m. A seven-pace by seven-pace room downstairs. A steel kitchen worktop immediately to your right as you enter. A bathroom-cum-toilet next to it. Another brown iron door opposite the entrance opened to the courtyard; but it was locked at that time.

I had stated at the prize ceremony in Strasbourg that my office had two windows, one giving on to the courthouse, and the other to a cemetery. The plastic desk I'd be working on here gave on to the wall. Specifically, the exercise courtyard's dirty yellow wall beyond the iron bars. And a little bit of black sky, shimmering like a stranger far, far away.

I opened the toilet door: as tiny as one you'd find in a petrol station. The shower was a step away from the squat toilet. And the washbasin, another step away, this time to the other side of the shower.

The mirror was taped to the wall. A strip bearing a logo was stuck to the toilet that looked none too clean; not one I'd want to step on. There was a two-inch gap between the iron door and the floor, and I could smell sewage.

'Thankfully I won't be staying long,' I said to myself, then laughed at my inner voice.

22 February 2016, *Bugün* newspaper

Twenty stairs led upstairs. There were three beds and three wardrobes. One of the beds had a mattress on it. On the bed lay a sheet, a pillow and a duvet cover. Duvets, however, were forbidden; instead, there was a brown blanket. Woven with a Turkish flag and a huge design: *Ministry of Justice/CTE/1923*.

CTE meant our host: *Ceza Tevkif Evleri*, that is, Penal Custody Homes – 'home' being a figure of speech in this context.

Just like the Ministry of Peace in Orwell's *1984* being responsible for war propaganda, our injustice dungeons wrapped you up in a blanket emblazoned with 'justice'... And that blanket looked desperately inadequate against the bitter cold of Silivri. To be fair, it wasn't as cold as I'd feared. But it was dim.

Two fluorescent strips on each floor cast a sick pallor on the dirty yellow walls, a shade that the inmate's countenance would soon adopt – a concern I had voiced in 2000, when we were touring the Sincan Type-F prison, then in construction, guided by the then Minister of Justice Hikmet Sami Türk. The prison he was waxing lyrical about was in fact a cemetery. A concrete catacomb where people are buried alive.

Duplex architecture, a wardrobe next to the bed or hot water twenty-four hours a day didn't transform that catacomb into a palace. What mattered was shackling the prisoner with unrelieved solitary confinement: an inhuman treatment intending to 'rehabilitate' the offender in practice sentenced the 'criminal' to solitude, a regimen devised to break the solidarity offered by a ward: isolated inmates capitulated more easily.

As might be expected, resistance wasn't long in coming: a hunger strike started in December 1999 in protest against the cells. Strikers were on the verge of death when several writers offered to mediate between the ministry and the activists.

Our group of writers and columnists meeting the striking prisoners included Yaşar Kemal, Orhan Pamuk, Mehmet Bekaroğlu, Zülfü Livaneli, Oral Çalışlar and Enver Nalbant.

I remember launching into negotiations in a ward immediately next to skin-and-bone strikers wearing a red headband, negotiations concerning whether they could survive, and what the conditions of any future prisoners would be.

December 1999, Bayrampaşa Prison. Yaşar Kemal,
Zülfü Livaneli, Orhan Pamuk, Can Dündar

They all said, 'Solitary means death.' They didn't trust the state. They claimed they could defend themselves in crowded wards, but should they be hanged in a cell, their deaths would have been brushed off as suicides.

They asked for alterations to the architecture of the Type-F

prisons to house at least twenty inmates per ward. Our negotiations at least convinced the state to create 'rooms' that
housed a maximum of seven inmates that opened up to one
another. But there still was a vast difference.

We had no idea the state was piling up outside as we were
busy with numbers. What ensued was a massacre instead of
an agreement. The greatest numbers of casualties in the history of prisons ensued: 122 dead and 400 wounded. That was
the savagery that broke the resistance. Isolation was legalised;
detention and deprivation converged.

I was now imprisoned by the same isolation that I, along
with several intellectuals, had tried to prevent fifteen years
earlier. As I stared at the empty yard beyond the bars in the
window, I wondered if that's where I would live. How long
would it last?

As I waited at the courthouse, I'd heard differing opinions:
'They'll detain you for a while, and then let you go…'; 'He's got
it in for you; he'll never let you go…'

I recalled what Deniz Gezmiş had said to his solicitor Halit
Çelenk: 'Once you're in the clutches of fascism…' A sentence
I repeated out loud. My voice wandered within the four bare
walls and echoed in my ears as if I'd yelled into a well. This was
the echo former inmates of Type-Fs referred to. Everything
resounded far more loudly inside. Water roared like a waterfall, and a door slammed like a thunderclap.

Solitude grew as fast as longing did. Lose hope and you'd be crushed like a rat in a trap. Especially if you weren't one of those who sought consolation in faith.

I removed my jacket, trousers and shirt. I placed them on one of the mattressless beds. I had no paper, no pen, nor book. I switched off the fluorescent light. Now light from the yard fell into the room, diced into a grid by the window bars that cast faint shadows on the beige floor tiles.

It looked like moonlight in the darkness. Good job I'd taught myself to dream, I thought…

Just as I had turned in, I heard voices from downstairs. The sound of conversation. I ran downstairs to take a look. Orhan Kemal was chatting with Nâzım Hikmet[19] at the table. Dostoyevsky was telling Cervantes about his time in the clink.

Aziz Nesin unfolded his plan for a new magazine at the window to show Sabahattin Ali, as Uğur Mumcu and İlhan Selçuk discussed the paper in another corner.[20] This was the haunt of activists against oppression, persecution and injustice around the world – the writer's library and the home of humankind, the mandatory stop of journalism, its privileged rank. Aware of this, I returned to bed, my mind at peace. Warmed by my rectitude.

I heard cheering in the distance, amongst sobs and the warders' whistles. The night was short. Morning nigh.

Hello, my palace of tears. Hello, my splendid isolation.

8

DAYTIME

LIFE BEGINS at 0715 with an ear-splitting whistle issuing from the telescreen in Big Brother's Oceania. Anyone who hears it is expected to be ready for Physical Jerks in three minutes.

Life begins at 0800 in tall brother's concentration camp with a sound issuing from the loudspeaker: 'Attention detainees and convicts! Morning roll call; please take your roll call positions.'

The loudspeaker ringing the reveille hangs above the door. Within three minutes of the announcement, a penitentiary protection squad unlocks the yard gate and checks if you're still there and if you're still alive.

You know 'you're counted'. Unlike being of account.

They enter the cell with a 'Selamünaleyküm'. The traditional 'Greetings to all' means 'Good morning' in Silivrish.

Also, 'Hello', 'You there?', 'Attention!' and 'Hey, you!', depending on context.

You are expected to come downstairs at once and show your face. This is also the one time to present any petitions you might have. Which I didn't know about on that first day, obviously.

I called out from my bed, having woken up from a good night's sleep, 'Good morning!', following the custom of my 'civilian life'. No reply. Given my circumstances, *good* and *morning* did sound pretty incongruous. I was still rubbing my eyes when four or five silhouettes in navy-blue uniforms climbed upstairs, looked at me, descended and exited, leaving the yard door open.

One called out, 'God save you' as they left.

'You too,' I replied. 'And us all…'

The cell now looked like a concrete matchbox, its tray pushed out. Above the tray was the sky: a leaden, lacklustre, sulking and distant sky… Angular, just like everything else here. A tetragonal firmament, as if it too was captive, caught between four walls.

Like a hen in a velvet jacket released from the coop, I stepped out into the yard called 'garden'. A sunless, soilless and flowerless garden enclosed by a thick wall that separated those who had surmounted the wall of fear. A ten-metre-high grimly yellow wall rising to cloudy skies, wearing a crown of barbed wire.

The familiar, vast, bright blue countenance of the sky was hemmed in between these wires; darkened, dull and overcast. Clouds of indeterminate intent seemed to be pressing down upon the yard.

That's when it occurred to me: Silivri was my 'Sky-Spotting Stop' as in the Turgut Uyar poem. I inhaled that handful of sky.

Our 'precious plot' was nine paces from one wall to the other, eight if you deduct the pivoting steps – hardly suitable for pacing. Every eight paces, you met a wall. The ground was damp enough for a coating of moss. A gully grate was sunk bang in the middle. Could one escape through it? Where did the sewer lead? Could I open a tunnel if I were to dig the toilet hole? Where would I hide the soil I'd dug?

Mahir and his mates had surreptitiously emptied the soil they'd dug out of their tracksuit pockets and socks onto the football pitch … [21]

But there wasn't an ounce of soil here, not even in a flowerpot. And the yard was far too small to mount a South American-style helicopter rescue. Best to shelve the idea of escape for a while then.

Erdem had to be beyond the wall, but it was impossible to hear or see him. I checked the door. There was an inspection window at forehead level, the size of a mobile phone. Like all windows, it, too, faced a wall. If you rose on tiptoe, you could see a few metres' worth of corridor.

This little window, designed more for peeping in rather than peering out, was placed just above an iron hatch that clearly only opened at mealtimes. I could have done with a cuppa.

Just as I was thinking this, I heard something in the yard. Like something had dropped in. But what could have dropped into the yard, when even birds avoided flying over it? I rushed out to take a look. Something wrapped in newsprint lay at the bottom of the wall. A small note was stuck on the parcel: 'Welcome!'

That's when I realised this was a gift sent from the neighbouring yard. I unwrapped it eagerly: three bright red apples emerged, clearly catapulted over the great barrier by a powerful arm, falling down from the skies just as in the folk tales of yore.

I was staring up into the air, trying to work out which direction it had come from, and who had lobbed it over, when a second parcel floated over the barbed wire and landed at my feet. A plastic soda bottle, again, wrapped in newsprint. And inside… – Yes! – piping hot tea, with some sugar cubes too.

My eyes were fixed heavenward, like the faithful anticipating another divine miracle, waiting to see what my mysterious neighbour would rain upon me next. This time it was a stentorian voice that slammed against the wall, not a parcel: 'Welcome, Can Abi…'

So someone knew I was here.

Hell is not the place you suffer; hell is the place no one hears you suffer.

So this wasn't the hell defined by the Sufi poet Mansour al-Hallaj.

I turned my mouth to the sky and yelled, 'Thank you, thank you, who are you?' He told me his name, but I couldn't make it out. The wall broke up the sounds. Then the deep voice suggested, 'Speak through the grate.'

Through the grate?

I bent down like a native American listening to the vibrations of the approaching stagecoach and put my ear to the grate.

'I'm Murat Çapan,' said the voice. '*Nokta*'s managing editor.'

He and his editor-in-chief Cevheri Güven had also been arrested on a charge of 'inciting rebellion' after a cover depicting – again – Erdoğan. They had been brought to Silivri a month before us. And here they were, using their seniority to lay on a welcoming party for us. Although we had never met, we had all fallen prey to the same oppression and had ended up as neighbours.

'The papers have covered your arrest in great detail – massive outrage. I heard protest marches would take place today,' said Murat.

What wonderful news! I yelled my thanks into the depths of the grate.

The editor-in-chief of a newspaper was trying to get the news from outside, communicating with the managing editor of a news magazine, both men speaking and listening in tandem … to a gully grate in the paved yard. The state of Turkish media in the twenty-first century.

Still, evidence that communication knows no bounds, bans, walls or obstacles. Just like water, sound finds a way to flow.

I saved one of the apples and tried to lob the other two to Erdem in the same way. Swinging my right arm as far back as I could, I attempted a hook shot, aiming at the clouds. In vain. My gift fell back without even reaching the barbed wire. And spilt out the apples too.

I obviously had to try much harder.

As I practised my catapulting technique, the greatest gift arrived from the other wall: that day's *Cumhuriyet…* Now that was a miracle. The detained journalist swapped places with the passionate journalist once again. The newsman had become the news.

Dilek Dündar's statement after the detention order

27 November 2015

'Media's Black Day' blared the headline on a black background. At the top, covering a quarter of the front page, was a photo of Dilek and me seated on the courthouse floor as we awaited the court order. *Souvenir of Çağlayan on a Wedding Anniversary.*

I was the only one smiling on that black page. I smiled again when I read of Dilek's reference to the trial of Danton: 'We stood firm. I ask everyone to stand firm,' she'd said after seeing me off to prison. 'We're hoping for good things,' she'd concluded.

I heard the voice of the mountain standing behind me in that yard. I stood straighter. Just then, the heavy iron hatch of the heavy iron door opened out and a mouth yelled in, 'Can Dündar!' – a call I would hear hundreds of times yet.

I leant down towards the hatch and locked eyes with the penitentiary enforcement officer calling my name. We started a bowed chat on either side of a door. I say 'chat', but it was more of an announcement rather than an exchange with a detainee, which was forbidden.

The young warder extended something: the canteen price list. On it 350 or so items were listed along with their prices. As I stared at it, he handed me a biro and a yellow notepad. It said 'Requisites Application Form'. You listed your requisites selected from the other list, noted the price and purchased them from the canteen – the mail order system of the pre-internet age.

And the money?

A visitor would deposit it. We were allowed to spend up to TL300 per week.[22] I asked for newspapers and a TV. He said I had to list them on the application form and then he shut the hatch. He had, quite unwittingly, just given me the world: pen and paper…

My two oldest friends were now with me.

I turned the requisites application form pad over, sat down by the blank pages and wrote my first piece.

9

WRITING

DEAR FRIEND,

Here we are again, together.

Whenever I'm in a pickle, you're the first one to take my arm; whenever I'm happy, you're the first one to hug me…

We've travelled so far together…

You have been my comrade, my confidant, my everything since that first day I put my first pen to my first sheet of paper.

My tongue, my school, my wound, my plaster.

You're the one who pinned my first red ribbon to my chest in primary school. You're the one who expressed the quickening of my blood, my first thrill as a youngster.

You it was who picked up my first love, and my last.

You it was who paid the first instalment of my first bookcase, and the mortgage on my latest house.

I shared the joy of my triumphs with you, and opened my wounded inner world to you when I was vanquished.

Came the day, my tears dissolved your ink, came the day, I put you on board a paper plane and launched you into the neighbour's garden.

Dissatisfied, I rubbed you out from time to time; but never out of my life…

I only did it to write better.

I rearranged the order of the words, like trying out rare objects in different parts of the home, the better to display you…

I sent you off to others, who received you with kisses and hugs.

I published you in books; they angered and were banned.

I wrote in newspapers; they were saved in clippings.

I wanted to be a biro at your service, one that never runs out of ink.

One of my favourite writers had once said, 'You can't live and write at the same time,' at a convivial dinner.

I took that as a maxim… I submitted to your jealousy.

I always picked you whenever the choice came between writing and living.

You were the draft of my life, sometimes leading, at others following.

Then you became my profession…

Fed me for years and years, paid me a salary.

My windfall and trapdoor too.

As you know, he who writes in this part of the world might well be writing his own verdict.

It is a foregone conclusion:

Authors of such and such sentences are shot.

Silence in the face of injustice is blessed with government favour.

This knowledge stifles some and stirs others, who are besotted with you...

As the first group cower in the fear corner, the second confront fear, you at their side.

And this time, you write the verdict for the authors of truth.

Which is precisely what you did with mine...

And now we're both locked up...

That's how it is in this country:

You're penned up the more you write, and write the more you're penned up.

And now I will write again, and you are going to drag me out of this well you threw me into. Now that I'm in the nick, you're going to reach out and grab me by the hand, by the arm just as you always had whenever I was in a pickle.

You will laugh and cry with me.

You will share my solitude.

You will write my solace and my defence.

You will put me on a paper plane and fly me off to the next

yard, to the world beyond the wire and walls, to freedom; you will reunite me with my loved ones.

Then you will return and dive into me again; you will scour the nooks and crannies and unearth whatever is hidden there.

Wounds, passions, fears and fights will only talk to you.

You will take notes.

You will carry them to tomorrow.

I'm so glad I chose you as my profession…

If I were an architect, engineer or carpenter, I'd have died of boredom.

But look, I carry you wherever I go, like a tortoise shell or a kangaroo joey…

I'm still flying on the wings you pinned on me at the age of eighteen… At times I talk to myself, at times touch a far distant heart with your help.

You're my interpreter, my psychologist, my weapon, my shield and my shoulder to cry on. You're my stimulant and sedative.

And now you're with me in the nick…

Look, it's just the two of us.

No one else…

Now write; be my tongue, my voice, my freedom and my power; write openly, no holds barred, galloping, dash off those lines, stark naked and fearless…

Show the world that no grave can bury a writer, that no working pen will run out of ink.

Encourage your friends...

Unnerve your foes.

10

SPY

'WELCOME, PATIENCE'.

That was the title of the first article I wrote for the *Cumhuriyet* in Silivri (28 November 2015), composed on the reverse side of the requisites application form in longhand, in the confusion of that first day…

I had written about the hearing, the road and my first hours at Silivri. The judge's vindictiveness, the police officers' courtesy and how far the prison was. I had no idea as yet how to get these notes out. Would I even be allowed?

There's a strange reality to being 'inside': you're taken captive, but are relieved of the dread of a raid on your home. And if you're facing a double life sentence, in particular, you abandon all discretion. You simply let go and write in torrents.

They think they've imprisoned you, but instead you're liberated. They want to gag you, but in doing so, they offer such a powerful platform that all ears turn to you and your voice is heard all the more. They lock you up between walls so that you can't look or see, but the peace inside allows you to see all the more clearly and gives you an even better bird's-eye view. They think they've blinded you, but your vision grows clearer.

The more they try to alienate and reduce you in solitary, the larger the number that believe you. Even if you were to be left all alone, 'like a stone at the bottom of the well' as Nâzım says, one part of you mingles with the crowds in the world.

They think they've 'buried you as deeply as they could' – and yes, they have. But prison transforms you into a seed – you burgeon instead of decomposing.

And that is the paradox of prison.

I was still writing when there was a commotion at the door. Silivri turned its hands to its latest guests. First came the canteen fellows who took my order. I needed a TV set above all, but I didn't have enough money on me. I had to wait for visitors to deposit some.

Then the librarian arrived, bringing a list of their books. Here was yet another old friend who'd come to the rescue. I asked for Dostoyevsky's *Notes from the Underground*, Victor Hugo's *The Hunchback of Notre Dame* and Stefan Zweig's *A Chess Story*. All those classics I hadn't touched for such a long time. This was an opportunity to be reunited with them.

Then came the 'custodian'. I had been divested of all my personal effects at reception: my wallet, my watch, pen, and wristband … Everything, down to the photo of Dilek and Ege in my wallet … My request to hang on to that last one was refused. The custodian who knocked on the door now had brought me this photograph. It was quite a courteous act under the circumstances. The souvenir of a happy day was extended through the hatch in the iron door, and the 'deposit' was received.

It was time for food.

The door's belly opened up once again and the hungry

prisoner heard a shout, 'Food!' The two plastic plates inside were extended. One returned with beans, the other with rice. And a third received pickles. The eye closed shut. I had my first meal as I wrote my first piece. But the traffic continued.

A warder came along, announcing I was to be taken for a medical check-up. The door opened. I was searched. We stepped out into the corridor, escorted by a warder in front and one behind. That's when I first noticed it: the large corridor was utterly deserted; or, more accurately, there was no one other than the penitentiary protection officers.

It was as if I was the only inmate of this concentration camp. I asked, but the warders looked reluctant to talk. They moved in total sobriety. It was the doctor who later explained the reason for the deserted state I had observed.

All detainees were made to wait while one passed in order to minimise the risk of an attack. Preventative measures had been tightened since the recent attack on Alaattin Çakıcı[23] in the corridor. So isolation wasn't going to be limited to the cell. We would be isolated inside the prison too.

The friendly doctor had come from Canada; he told me there were a total of 15,000 detainees and convicts at the Silivri campus. So I was sharing a concentration camp with 15,000 men. Yet, if they were all to be taken away in the night, I'd never know.

I was placed in extreme solitary where I would feel totally

alone. To the extent that I wouldn't be able to even see Erdem's face, and he was no farther than two steps away.

The doctor asked if I had any medical issues. I didn't, except for a dental treatment that had started a while back. It never occurred to me that the orthodontic treatment I'd begun half-heartedly would be a lifesaver at Silivri. The doctor said he'd write to Çapa for the continuation of this treatment, and I would be taken there on certain days of the week. So I could go out 'by the skin of my teeth …' A door had opened on the very first day.

Then it was the psychologist's turn. Any detainee who wanted to take an interview could, although it wasn't mandatory. I said, 'Yes, I would like to,' out of curiosity. Everything was new for me, everything added to my knowledge.

They led me to a room where I sat down facing two young interviewers. Very politely, they said they had a few questions to ask. They asked my name, age and profession. And why I was imprisoned…

'Terror or criminal?'

I leant back and, emboldened by the questioning at admission, offered a perfunctory, 'I'm a spy,' said in the air of a James Bond as I enjoyed the astonishment this aroused in my interlocutors.

That astonishment substantiated the absurdity of the allegation. I was accused of espionage, but since no country was named, I had no idea who was my boss. I'd have asked for an exchange on a bridge with one of theirs if I did.

And because I was such a novice at this espionage business, I had spread the first bit of information I'd received all over the front page of a newspaper, instead of passing it on to the secret service. And I was obviously caught on my first mission.

The only proof of my espionage was that news report in the paper. And I was locked up so I couldn't tamper with the evidence.

Since the print run was 100,000 that day, there were 100,000 pieces of evidence. In order to tamper with that evidence, I would have had to gather every single copy and black out the headlines. I was arrested in order to prevent me doing so.

An elegant young lady joined the interviewers and explained courteously that it was their duty to go through a set of questions.

'No problem, go ahead,' I said.

One concerned who had pushed me into crime.

My mother had.

When I was still a baby, she had started reading books to me, whether I understood a word or not; by raising my awareness, she had prepared me for crime.

Oh yes… Then there was my primary school teacher.

By teaching me how to write, she had equipped me with the instrument of crime.

'Are you going to continue to commit crime after your release?' she posed quite diffidently.

'So it seems,' I replied. 'I can't stop reading or writing…'

They asked no more. We ended the interview without finishing the set.

In the meantime, thousands were gathering outside the newspaper headquarters as colleagues marching and chanting slogans in Ankara were gassed by the police.

Except Şişli's voice had yet to reach Silivri. For that, I needed a relatively newer friend in comparison to paper, pen and books: I needed a TV set.

Visibility

11
VISIBILITY

IF THERE were a unit of measure called 'visibility', it would be sixty paces in Silivri. The 'Visit Room' is sixty paces away, you see…

The iron hatch in the door opens. A voice reaches in: 'Can Dündar? Got a solicitor.' Or, 'Can Dündar? MP visit.'

This means, 'Get ready.' You change from tracksuit and trainers into something a little more formal. Exchanging anything with your solicitor is subject to approval. You can't take even a pen with you.

My outfit was perfectly adequate in the formality stakes on the first day. 'Got a solicitor' sounded quite thrilling. This was my first visitor.

The door opened. I was searched. We went through that unlovely scenario of removing shoes, tapping heels on the floor, putting them back on and lacing them back up again. I entered the corridor, escorted by two warders.

Two iron grille doors stood one after the other. Until you opened one and entered the gap between the two, the next remained firmly shut. Once we were through, we were also done with the sixty paces. We had arrived at the legal visit hall: glass cubicles arranged in a row rather like a train, each with a divider at waist height, flanked by two plastic chairs. One for visitors, one for the inmate. All visits took place inside this aquarium, under the watchful eye of the warders.

My first visitor was Metin Feyzioğlu, Chairman of the Union of Bar Associations.

'Hug me like your wife,' he smiled when he saw me. 'Just don't go too far…'

This was the glass cubicle in which I'd entertain over 200 lawyers in the coming weeks. Demirel's promise from way back when hadn't been kept: police station walls weren't transparent. Instead, the defence rooms that ought to be private had become transparent. Feyzioğlu put his considerable law experience to explain the illegality of our detention. He added, 'I will discuss this with the Prime Minister.' He cheered me up and left.

Out of the room, and then another body search…

Remove shoes. Right one first… Bang the heel on the floor, and put it back on. Then the left… Bang the heel on the floor, and put it back on. Walk. Take sixty steps. By the cell. Halt.

Another body search.

Remove shoes. Right one first… Bang the heel on the floor, and put it back on. Then the left… Bang the heel on the floor, and put it back on.

All you've walked is sixty paces, and the whole of that time escorted by the warders. Why would you be searched again? You know it's to wear you down.

'Why?' you ask.

'Orders,' they reply. 'We're just following orders.'

Fine: change the orders, and you change the ones following them. Which is why your struggle is with the order, and not with the follower.

I stepped into the cell. The hatch opened: 'Can Dündar? MP visit.'

Door, search, shoes, right/left, walk…

This time to the right of the corridor. MPs are seen in the open visit hall, where there is no barrier between visitor and inmate. This is a hall evoking images of freedom, where pictures of horses and nature hang on the walls. You can chat for up to an hour, sitting on plastic chairs. And since the visitor is an MP, you even get a cup of tea.

My first MP visitors were Utku Çakırözer, Şafak Pavey, Mustafa Balbay and Candan Yücer. They'd all come to offer their support as well as to bring Kılıçdaroğlu's letter of 'congratulations'.

l to r: Şafak Pavey, Mustafa Balbay, Candan Yücer and Utku Çakırözer

As I hugged Balbay, I said, 'My watch now.' I had visited him when he was incarcerated in Sincan. At the time he'd told me about the difficulty of writing longhand since he wasn't given a typewriter inside: the right hand grew numb after a while, and he had taught his left hand to write.

That's what stuck in my mind most out of that one-hour visit. It was my lazy left hand's turn to take the writing course. Balbay gave me other practical tips as an 'old lag'...

'Look after your health. Try not to catch a cold.'

'Make sure you work out. The yard is short; if you go back and forth, you eventually sprain your ankles. Best to keep a circular path. At least for an hour...'

'Don't try to wash your clothes by hand. Put it in the plastic bowl and trample on it. "Heel-o-matic" washes really well.'

'The food is really greasy. Rinse it first, then reheat it in the kettle.'

It was all highly valuable advice, but I had no bowl or kettle as yet.

Balbay was my Silivri Home Secretary that day. And Utku was the Foreign Secretary.

Utku, my predecessor at the paper, was a CHP European Council Parliamentary Assembly member, and therefore experienced in relations with Europe. He was our support throughout our incarceration, tirelessly visiting us and carrying our voice to the world.

He spoke of massive outrage around the world: 'Foreign media has covered it extensively. *#WeAreArrested* is a worldwide trending topic on Twitter. The US Ambassador blacked out his Instagram account. Reporters Without Borders have declared you a "hero". They've started a petition for your release.'

He reminded us of the upcoming Turkey–European Union Summit in Brussels scheduled for Sunday: 'It might make sense to send a message there.'

The reason the EU had suddenly remembered Turkey after all this time and had convened a summit with Prime Minister Davutoğlu was the refugees swarming their borders. They were going to ask Ankara to establish a concentration camp to keep the refugees in check in exchange for €3 billion. Human rights and the freedom of the press could sink into insignificance when confronted with the fear of a flood of refugees. All the same, it was worth a try.

I promised Utku I'd write.

I also handed him the column I'd written on the reverse side of the requisites application form and asked him to get it to the newspaper.

As soon as I had returned to my cell, I took his advice and started writing to European leaders who would attend the summit. The requisites application form pad I'd been using to write my newspaper column provided the paper for letters to Europe this time.

I wrote a letter to Merkel...

A letter to Hollande...

A letter to Renzi...

A letter to Cameron...

To twenty-eight leaders in total, hoping their sensitivity concerning the refugee crisis would not stand in the way of their principles on human rights.

I turned the pad over once the letters were done and started writing a list of requisites from the canteen: a pitcher for the squat toilet, a mop for the floor...

I was suddenly struck by the hilarity of listing a toilet pump on the reverse of a letter to the President of the EU Council. It was tough, this spying business... But it was better than stealing.

Notes from prison

Two lawyers came to visit in the afternoon: my old friend Tunç Soyer and our dear solicitor Bülent Utku. Tunç and I had shared so many ups and downs over the years; we'd even raised our children together. Now he was in his barrister robes, visiting his friend in detention – a huge morale boost.

'You'll come out of here much stronger,' he said. 'There were claims that you wouldn't risk prison. That you'd run away to sip wine in Europe. They were stunned too.'

Bülent Utku, for his part, told me about the huge demonstration outside the newspaper offices earlier that morning. The newspaper was also up in arms.

'On Monday, we'll appeal against your detention: we'll go to the Constitutional Court. If that doesn't work, then we'll go to the European Court of Human Rights.'

They asked me what I needed and wanted.

I wanted my Twitter account to be kept open. I would continue to send messages, stories and comments from inside.

I had made my mind up: I would transform this dungeon into a microphone, make my voice heard as far as it could reach.

12

DİLEK

WIM WENDERS tells the story of a man in search of his wife in *Paris, Texas*, my favourite amongst his films.

The film opens on this half-deranged, scruffy fellow wandering in the desert, a red baseball cap over a head full of shaggy hair and scraggly beard. Nearing the end of the film, he finds his wife in a peep-show. They're in two small cabins separated by a window. She cannot see the 'client'.

The client gets to watch: he would tell her on the phone what he wants her to do, and she would perform. She soon realises it's her own husband on the other end. And that phone call turns into a heart-breaking reckoning.

That, to me, is one of the most unforgettable scenes in cinema.

What we're watching in this age of communication is the lack of communication between two people who should have been closest; they're sitting on either side of a pane of glass and on either side of a telephone.

It's not just the glass that separates them.

This scene popped into mind when Dilek came for a 'closed visit' on Friday evening.

The closed visit room was situated immediately opposite the legal visit hall. In contrast to those cubicles, here you were separated by two thick panels of glass. I was bursting with excitement when I dived in.

We leapt up as if we hadn't seen each other for months. Our palms kissed on either side of the window; the kiss of fingers left their mark on the glass… Lifting the handsets, we started a relaxed chat.

She looked very elegant, strong and determined. Without the slightest hint of sadness, resignation or anxiety. She was cheerful and brave. The magnificent METU Student Council firebrand girl that surfaced at times of crisis was born again.

Earlier in the day, she had addressed the crowds outside the newspaper: 'Another badge of honour on the *Cumhuriyet*'s chest… I'm sure everyone is proud.'

She, who always avoided putting herself forward, who always hid in the background, had yelled out when the occasion called for it. The unfair seesaw of living with a writer:

'Lower yourself when he rises – as if it's not you raising him! – and rise up and shout if he crashes to the ground.'

She rattled off a heap of news: reverberations outside, friends rushing over to help and our mothers' tears… She spoke of how she consoled countless callers on the phone and filling our home, and told them to show their reaction instead of merely feeling sad.

For years our telephone had been bugged; but this time the police were listening openly, officially. So we enjoyed this openness…

The state was in the glass between us and the handsets in our hands. And it was now visible. At least we no longer had to worry I might be run in at any time. Now we could poke fun.

'I'll grow my beard until acquittal if that's all right with you,' I said with a smile.

'I'd guessed as much,' she said. She had been objecting to a beard for quite a while, but now I had a reasonable excuse.

She said she'd brought over the books I'd set aside before leaving – and added a few of her own favourites.

The telephone's beep alerted us that the hour – that had gone in a flash – was up. I showed her the tiny passport photo I'd secreted in my pocket. A photo taken in a tiny cubicle not much different from this one, Ege between the two of us. A photo full of wide grins.

She looked; her eyes filled. We gazed at each other, our words muted.

The line was cut. We left.

I went back.

The TV set arrived – the most powerful antidote to my loneliness after pen, paper and books… The generator that powers the prisoner. Tunç had deposited the money and the luminous box of hope, a veritable 29-channel spaceship landing in the medieval décor, brightened up the dark cell.

A new window was on my table this time; I could see those within, but they couldn't see me. But they were calling out as though they did.

'Freedom!' they shouted.

'Justice!' they yelled.

'They're not alone!' exclaimed their banners.

The bare walls that echoed and magnified every sound amplified these slogans too. My heart swelled with the crowd pouring into the cell from the screen. So I wasn't alone on this path I would stay on even if I were left all by myself.

I murmured, 'Risk loneliness if you want to grow into a crowd.'

I channel hopped, delighted like the first time we had a TV when I was a child. I looked for friends amongst the marchers; spotted them, touched their sad faces… I accompanied their slogans… I was gassed along with the demonstrators in the capital.

28 November 2015

Reports of Deputy Prime Minister Numan Kurtulmuş's statement, 'They're not charged with journalism, but the principle is no pre-trial detention,' made me smile.

The statement issued by the Prosecutor's office, alarmed at the reaction, 'This investigation has nothing to do with freedom of the press,' made me laugh out loud.

Cumhuriyet columnists Tayfun Atay and Ayşe Yıldırım Başlangıç, and my solicitor Tora Pekin were debating on IMC TV.

Ayşe said, 'This is a turning point… A milestone… The support we saw today has to continue. This solidarity must continue.' She wanted to see more in support demonstrations than a brief flash. This was a marathon.

The warm breath of solidarity reached all the way from Şişli to Silivri and warmed my room.

28 November 2015, the police pepper spraying
demonstrators in Ankara

'You're not alone.'

This was the good news that would help every captive cling
to life. And had put its arm through mine that first night.

They'd have a hard time putting me down now.

13

CURSE

ON SATURDAY morning, *Cumhuriyet* sent me a press digest. The *Akit* ran the following:

> We'd like to point to a detail in the Can Dündar affair and ask: How long have Can Dündar and his spouse Dilek Dündar been married for?
>
> According to Dilek Dündar, the day Can Dündar was arrested, that is, the other day, it was their twenty-eighth wedding anniversary.
>
> I was curious enough to check; has it really been twenty-eight years since their wedding?
>
> The news claim: 'They were married in 1991.'
>
> Fine, but then, wouldn't they have been married for twenty-four years, and not twenty-eight?

[...]

Since Dilek Dündar mentions twenty-eight years, the couple ought to have been wed in 1987. Yet records state '1991'.

Oh, yeah... Can Dündar also has a son named Ege Dündar.

Ege was born in 1989...

Wouldn't you want to ask then; Is Ege Dündar, the son of Can and Dilek Dündar? Is he another woman's son? Or is he the fruit of a pre-marital relationship?

The article carried on in this vein. Yet another example of the below-the-belt mudslinging we'd got used to... If I were out, I'd have laughed it off with a 'What's it to you, chief?' Or texted him: 'You've been conned: we got married in '88 and Ege was born in '95.'

But when you're inside, and if you've only just been banged up, you might be excused for a sense-of-humour failure. The heart might be just that little bit more fragile; rage: a spear ready to lash out at any moment.

I was upset. Perhaps by the crudity or the depravity that kicks a man when he's down...

And perhaps... (I hope Dilek will forgive me for this revelation) because Ege was our blessing after three miscarriages.

Whatever... What could I do? I couldn't send in a correction request; I cursed instead.

My mouth full of rage, whipped up by hatred, with a

protective instinct, I yelled curses at the walls, the heavens and the city, stunning myself with my rage and fury... I'd never seen myself like this. I couldn't recognise myself for a while.

Then I simmered down. Like I did every time I got angry, I waited for the storms inside to abate, and reined in the ferocious stallion rearing up. I calmed down. It passed. And I forgot about it a few hours later.

Later...

Five weeks went by after the publication of this comment. I was writing to Ege after New Year, asking if this topic had upset him.

My desk was immediately next to the radiator, by the window to the yard. My hand felt tired momentarily, and I turned my head to look at the TV on top of the fridge. A breaking news ticker tape caught my eye.

I couldn't believe my eyes. The author of that comment... had died.

He had been in the pink of health and yet had died suddenly of a heart attack. I was scared. Afraid of the power of my rage. I blamed the curse I'd blown at the skies.

My jaw dropped as though I had unwittingly committed a murder, as though I were accountable for the sudden death... My grandma whispered into my ear just then, 'God is great, son.' I forgot what he'd written, and was upset.

'God forgive his sins,' I said towards the heavens.

When our doyen journalist Metin Toker was imprisoned in the 1950s, he'd prayed, 'God, don't let me come out full of vengeance.'

Vengefulness thrives on the dungeon floor. You need patience to bury it deep, replace it with the grace of resignation and draw strength from your innocence.

Innocence has a quiet strength. Innocence has a strength that isn't afraid of the dark, isn't afraid to speak its mind, needs no other power for support and isn't cowed by threats. Unnoticed when the waters rise. But once the storm has stilled, the floodwaters wash away slander, expletives, hatred and anger. All that is left behind is innocence that quietly resists injustice and burrows deep to hide from the iniquity of the shallows...

And this is known as 'divine justice'.

Which I trust.

14

TIME

OUTSIDE, THE weekend is a welcome break. Inside, it's the opposite...

Silivri goes to sleep on Saturdays and Sundays. Time that gushes like a waterfall on visit days trickles like still waters once the week is done. The minute hand is lazy, the hour hand indolent...

The voices fall silent, the canteen is shut, and traffic dies down. The gloom of a deserted public office settles into the corridors. Time is not measured in hours, at any rate. Roll call, newspaper, bread, food, pacing – that's how you know what time it is.

The cell is a waiting room: you wait for the papers to come, for the bread, for the yard door to be unlocked, for the meal, for the evening, for a match on TV, for night, for morning.

But most of all, for release.

For discharge, for deliverance and for freedom…

'When?' always connects to the same point: 'When do we get out?'

The days and hours are counted in similar routines:

Telephone day.

Visit day.

Sports day.

Post day.

Cargo day.

A routine that surreptitiously 'convicts' you. Forces you into a lifer's psychology even before your trial. The scratches you place in some hidden corner of the wall turn into iron bars as they grow in number. The duration of your wait becomes your dungeon.

On that first Saturday, I naturally had no idea about any of this. All I could guess was that I would be spending some time in this boring trap. As someone who always preferred surprises to routines, I felt the need to cope with the monotony first of all.

I decided to break the imposed routine. My first act of resistance would target monotony.

I showered off the gloom conferred by the above-mentioned newspaper. That charmless toilet-cum-bathroom could be transformed into a steam bath provided you ran the hot water for a couple of minutes – and exercised your imagination. And the bare walls offered a magnificent stage for shower singers.

The breakfast planned for 8 a.m. could wait. I prepared my first brunch at Silivri: a Mediterranean salad of tomatoes and peppers, topped with feta, oregano and olive oil… Butter and jam… And my first tea in the brand-spanking new pot.

The feast was ready. But the venue looked a bit dull. And a cool wintry sun smiled outside. I decided to 'eat out' that day. I carried the white plastic table to the yard. Placed it bang in the middle, right above the grate. I spread the duvet cover, a makeshift tablecloth. I took out my breakfast. Poured the tea. Put on my jumper and bomber jacket. I folded the blanket into a cushion for the plastic chair.

There was still something missing.

Of course! Music!

The 29-channel TV's channel 21 was tuned to Dream TV. I brought the TV set as close to the yard window as I could and turned the volume all the way up. Well, well, well! The empty yard had turned into a roaring loudspeaker. Silivri rang out.

Adele Weekend was on. And that's where I first heard the song 'Hello' – there, on that day, in that yard. I was enchanted. I took a break from breakfast and asked myself to dance. I closed my eyes and danced, shaded by steel wire. Dancing was a skill that you could take anywhere you went, just like writing. Convenient, undemanding, entertaining... Took my breath away. Hugged and flung me beyond the thick walls. It reunited me with my loved ones.

It had been years since I last danced with such emotion. I hope the warders watching the yard were equally impressed. Great if they were gobsmacked – 'Bloke's dancing 'cos he's banged up!'

The next routine to break was sleep. I decided to change the time and place. The iron bedstead was screwed to the floor, but the mattress was not. I heaved it on my back and lugged it downstairs. During this move, I accidentally knocked the loud-speaker over the door. (And thereby spared myself any further noise pollution in the form of unsolicited announcements.)

I laid out the mattress in the nook under the staircase, beyond the range of the spyhole in the door. Plastic bowl overturned at my feet as a stand, the blanket pulled over my knees, I had a terrific TV corner.

I had made a home out of the dungeon. I grabbed a book and lay down for my first siesta. Noon would be the new time for sleep – nights would be for working.

I liked becoming the lord of the rules of my little cell. I had no watch, but I had time. Time like I'd never had before.

Dilek had brought me *Red Time*,[24] which opens with a fairy tale told by Mine Söğüt's grandma when the author was little:

Children too young to perceive time had the capacity to

sense that divine infinity. This made them peaceful and fear-less. Since they couldn't perceive time, they couldn't perceive the passage of time either, and so thought they were immortal.

Her grandma had added, 'Now you're still enjoying that enchanted perception of boundless time. You'll grow up when you notice the passage of time.'

As I read these lines under the stairs in a silent nick, wrapped in a blanket (prison-issue one), I felt I was enjoying the enchanted perception of boundless time.

That terrifying race with time was left outside the great door.

I was a child once again…

At peace.

And fearless.

15

PACING

GUNSHOTS ROUSED me from a peaceful siesta. The screen was awash with blood.

Shot bang in the middle of Diyarbakır, 'The Peace Envoy' was stretched out on the ground. As familiar as the poet had said, 'I'd recognise that gunshot anywhere.' The work of our dark streets. TV stations conveyed Elçi's final tweet. He'd written about us: 'That arrest is the greatest blow to freedom of press and expression. Without a violent social reaction, it'll be hard to escape from that dark tunnel of no return.'

Immediately afterwards, that tunnel of no return had dragged him into its own darkness. We were the last victims he'd defended: Erdem, I and the Four-Pillar Minaret.[25]

My old friend Tayfun Atay's column that day could have been written about Tahir Elçi and not me.

Tayfun reminded me of the lines I'd written after my deceased lecturer Ünsal Oskay. 'The Master' would speak for three extraordinary periods non-stop, with no breaks, in those legendary lectures of his attended by a breathless audience; he'd speak of dreams of a noble life, no alienation, and bring the topic round to Herman Melville's *Moby Dick*. As he read page after page with a trembling chin, wiping away tears with the back of his right hand, he'd say: 'This is a tale of mankind's noble resistance... The only losers are the pioneers. They suffer, yet they are the ones who pave the way.'

Tahir Elçi lay in the middle of the way he'd hewn with the pickaxe of pain. Just like Hrant Dink[26] had. As if he could raise everyone else if he lay down.

So I flung myself out into the concrete garden. I started pacing. Like I was taught: touring in an oval in the rectangular yard, and banging into the same wall at each corner, I walked in the cold as if wandering in the treacherous history of the land filled with culs-de-sac.

The moss on the ground was like a festering wound, defying imagination that tries to replace it with a lawn ... The sky was pale, sunless and dull.

A deep ache in my heart coming from Diyarbakır, I started pacing inside my concrete box like an angry lion in his cage...

One, two, three, four, turn...

One, two, three, four, five, six, seven, eight, turn...

One, two, three, four, turn…

One, two, three, four, five, six, seven, eight, turn…

My steps growing increasingly faster, increasingly more violent, flinging me from one wall to the next.

The more you're constrained, the more you're prodded to break through those constraints. You walk, your longing for freedom alongside… Along with mad ideas, new essays, deep memories and dreams of a walk without walls…

Your footsteps echo in your ear… And the rustle of the black plastic bag on the barbed wire, the packaging of an old compass fluttering like a Jolly Roger.

A molten sky overhead. As if it, too, is captive: pierced by neither aircraft nor birds. The sun does not descend, the moon does not rise. You'd never know it if the wind blew or a cloud scudded past. So untrustworthy a sky, so alien.

The Czech writer Julius Fučik asks in notes smuggled out before he was hanged, 'How many prison cells has humankind paced before it could progress, I wonder? And how many more it has to pace…'

Until that noble dream comes true.

Just think about it.

One, two, three, four, turn…

One, two, three, four, five, six, seven, eight, turn…

16

EGE

THE HATCH opened. The warder called my name: 'Can Dündar? Got a letter.'

I had put my address at the bottom of the column I'd sent the paper, and added, 'Anyone who wants to write to me is welcome.' The first letter I received was placed into my palm like a white dove bearing glad tidings. The writing on the envelope was that familiar scrawl…

Date: 28 November 2015. A stamp in the corner:

The Silivri Penitentiaries Letter Reading Commission – Checked

I took it and went upstairs. Stretched out on a bed to enjoy my grief. The greeting made me burst into tears straight-away:

SİLİVRİ KAPALI CEZA
İNFAZ KURUMU MEKTUP
OKUMA KOMİSYONU
GÖRÜLMÜŞTÜR

28 Kasım 2015

Dear Dad,

I thought I'd write a letter, but did wonder if you could cope with my handwriting in the middle of all your troubles. Plus the spelling mistakes! Please forgive me.

What a weird world this is, some punter's drawn walls and wires between us … The Bosphorus is the same Bosphorus … Your papers, pen, text of that last speech in France, an empty Zegna box, and your absence …

We might be standing upright, OK, still, I'm not gonna hide how much I miss you … 'Don't worry,' I tell myself, 'he'll fetch up in the fresh light of some morning, maybe in the winter, maybe in the spring, maybe in the middle of his favourite season … We'll spoon the Nutella again, watch a match, pour our grief out to each other, grow up together … And even maybe, we'll give some wreck of a Cadillac some stick and tear up Highway 61 … BB King screams again, "Thrill is gone!" as we gallop in the car towards the heart of the sun, like two cowboys…'

Dear Dad, don't you worry… I know you won't, but never lose hope. The future is on our side. I miss you like mad, but don't miss you at all. Because you are in the pride that overflows my rib cage, in the endless ink of my pen, in twenty years' worth of memories of our friendship, and in the guide in my heart on this long road that is life. The greatest privilege of my life has been your hands I felt holding the back of my bike in every adventure I embark upon… Even if you'd already let go as I pedal towards the horizon, even if you're already watching confidently…

So you see Dad, neither walls nor death can separate us… You're in my self-confidence and the tone of my voice.

To cut a long story short, read and write, write and read. Make fun of everything like you always manage to, and defy the days they've laid out in front of you.

And never forget:

No wall in this world can deny our love or our words from each other… We won't lose either. Because we've never chased victory. What could possibly be more noble, more meaningful than speaking the language of this wind, this sun, these lovely seasons, love, old friendships, longing, sorrow, boundless oceans and waves and the silent demesne of the stars?

Never mind those who choke on their own venom... We, our family, we are closer than ever before, safer than ever before, in the temple of our smile...

Dear Dad, I am proud to be your son and honoured to be your friend. I can't wait for the day when we'll meet again.

I kiss your hands and eyes.

Your son,

Ege.

A very dear friend had once given me some therapy advice: 'Don't be ashamed to bend if you're punched. If you insist on standing straight, your internal organs might be damaged. Best to just buckle under the pain and straighten up later.'

I took that advice on that day. I let go of the lump I'd been harbouring in my throat for months, and I buckled. I sobbed and sobbed for the first time in an unscheduled resistance break. With longing... with pride... and sorrow... and pleasure...

Sometimes, when you're alone, you have to lick your wounds like a stray dog, and patch your spirit.

I licked and patched, sinking over two white sheets...

I watched Ege the following evening with journalist Mirgün Cabas on CNN Türk. I settled into my plastic chair and stared at him like an artist looking at the painting he's just finished. Having isolated his father from his hero, he was saying,

'I'm proud and honoured on behalf of Can Dündar, and angry and sad on behalf of my dad.'

I felt proud and honoured on behalf of Ege, and angry and sad on behalf of my son…

17

SOLITARY

[In solitary confinement] you lived like a diver under a bell in the dark ocean of that silence; like a diver who guesses that the cord to the world above has torn free and that he will never be hauled back up out of the noiseless deep. There was nothing to do, nothing to hear, nothing to see, everywhere and always there was nothing around you, a complete and timeless and spaceless void.

[…]

This actually indescribable state of affairs lasted for months. Now – four months, that's easily jotted down: less than a dozen letters. […] But no one can recount, can measure, can communicate, not to anyone else, not to himself, how long a time in a spaceless, timeless place really lasts, and to no one can you explain how this corrodes and consumes you, this nothing and nothing and nothing around you, this always-the-same-table-and-bed-and-washbasin-and-wallpaper, and always this silence, always the same warder who pushes in the food without looking, always the same thoughts circling around in the void until you start to go mad.[27]

Stefan Zweig had written these lines a few months before his suicide in 1942. The Nazi dungeon he relates in *A Chess Story* was like the Silivri of 2015. The same oppression, the same solitary.

When he's taken for interrogation, the prisoner in *A Chess Story* notices a book in the overcoat pocket of one of the torturers, sneaks it out with shaking hands and, concealing it under his belt, carries it back to his cell, his knees trembling all the while. This is a book on chess; a book that would become a lifebelt for the prisoner, rescuing him from his hell and transforming him into a chess master.

The book considered as Zweig's farewell letter accompanied me one Silivri night. When they came round for the evening roll call, they thought I was in my cell; I, on the other hand, was playing chess on the steamship to Buenos Aires.

The book that recounted the story of a book that helps a lonely concentration camp prisoner cling to life was, three quarters of a century later, and in another concentration camp, dragging another lonely prisoner from hell.

The loyalty, light and companionship of a book that reaches beyond the ages... And of course, its power to keep humans and humankind alive and transform.

This power heartens the imprisoned and terrifies the imprisoner. That is why writing and writers are in the firing line, are censored and imprisoned.

That is why they not only imprison you, but also try to isolate you, something I pondered for a good long while when I was in solitary in Silivri. Countless masters of our literature and arts were trained and matured in dungeons, and transformed their jails into academies, studios and production centres.

Nâzım's *Human Landscapes from my Country* was inspired by the characters the poet had met inside. As were the characters in Yılmaz Güney's *Road*...

Ruhi Su's songs, Kemal Tahir's novels and Sabahattin Ali's poems all carry traces and echoes of their time behind bars. The characters they had drawn were as real, as tangible as they themselves were, since they'd all shared a prison room and the same troubles.

The first time you're allowed to go out into the sun on a Sunday is such a boost to the morale, the bitter cold that seeps in through the unglazed window freezes you to the bone, the smell of the spring onion brought by a visitor and the coal store that heralds the arrival of autumn in Mamak... all this, and more, we learnt from prison literature.

Being a prisoner was tough: the conditions were hard and the terms long. But this was shared punishment… The inmates of the ward helped one another, cooked and ate together. When one buckled under the weight of longing, all paced and sang together to lift the spirit; when troubles reared up, all cursed together heavenwards. Every Deniz made fun, every Mahir played football. Defences were written together, tunnels were dug together and the self-styled scrivener – the poet of the ward – would pen letters for them all.

That is what made life behind bars the mine of humanity that inspired the writer in creating characters and plots. Enabled the writer to cut the gem he found then and there, turn it into a poem, a novel, a painting or a short story on the spot.

Just think about the blossoming and cascading of Orhan Kemal's pen under Nâzım's tutelage when they were banged up together. Prisons were schools of literature in their own right…

Just as 'you ain't marrying my daughter unless you've done your national service', 'you ain't calling yourself a writer unless you've done your bit behind bars'. The walls of the old prisons still rang with the voices, traces and words of the greatest masters of these lands.

But…

Then came the day when the state noticed this. Whoever went in came out better equipped. Instead of merely being released, they were graduating, filling in the gaps in their career.

Not only was the ward not a home of reform, it was actually a training centre, stoking the rebellion earmarked for quashing. Nothing worked any longer, no rough beating, torture or the strappado. So another method was needed to crush the prisoner.

They discovered solitary confinement.

They dispensed with the ward system and locked the 'criminal' up in small cells. The main torture, though, was the isolation.

Twentieth-century tales of prison, songs of warders and drawings of pacing all came to an end with the twenty-first. The state stuffed the captive in its hands into the F-type isolation and transformed one meaning of punishment into the other, into torment. Concrete cells were built behind thick walls and contact between convicts was severed.

Now the buildings are modern, the warders are smartly turned out and there is running hot water... The bitter cold is no longer freezing, and the food arrives cooked. But human contact is forbidden.

The bread is handed out through the hatch in the iron door, but chatting with the 'penitentiary protection officer' is forbidden...

When you're escorted to a visit, other inmates are kept waiting; chance encounters are forbidden...

Your loved ones are behind a thick pane of glass at visit; 'kith and kin together,' yes, but touching is forbidden...

If your visitor brought you some spring onions, you wouldn't receive them; bringing them in is forbidden…

You'd never know if the coal depot were to be emptied; the other side of the wall is forbidden…

Footballs are sold at the canteen, but you can only play against the wall; forming a team is forbidden…

You want to write a novel, a poem or your own defence? Typewriters were free for Nâzım in the 1940s, for Deniz in 1971 and for Ecevit[28] in 1981, but for you in the 2000s? Forbidden…

The windows are double-glazed now, but you're constantly under observation; curtains are forbidden…

You have a 'garden' of your own… devoid of flowers: soil is forbidden…

You're expected to circle round and round like an ocean fish stuck in a bowl and suffocate in the smoke of your own blues. Isolation tries to 'discipline' you and bring you to your knees by leaving you alone with yourself.

The wisdom of the twenty-first century state has replaced the fecund prison of the previous century with stone catacombs, and thereby not only extinguished a tradition, but also its art, poetry, literature, painting and songs.

It would not be unreasonable to envisage a preponderance of poems of self-reflection in the prison literature of the new century.

This means:

A guerrilla war with loneliness awaits you inside. You are your only companion. You will defeat this dungeon on your own, create a verdant forest inside yourself in this darkness.

You run a high risk of injury if you're at war with yourself...

Your potential to benefit is high if you're at peace with yourself...

In the dead of the night, when you're left alone with yourself, you realise you'd been neglecting yourself for quite a while, hadn't chatted or opened up for quite a while.

If your natural disposition favours taciturnity towards yourself, if you're boring company, you've had it.

If you can replicate yourself, if you can guide your spirit away from thorny paths into entertaining lanes, you're fine.

This is a process of holding a mirror inside yourself; if what you see is dark, it will only depress you all the more. If it's bright, it will brighten up your cell. Never mind stuffing you inside the dungeon, it will pull you out, out, out.

C'mon, let's have a game of chess now...

18

VILLA

OUR INCREASINGLY frequent complaints about isolation must have troubled the ministry. Instead of approving local and foreign delegation visit requests, it settled on a far more fail-safe method.

It ordered the *Bugün* newspaper (now under 'administrative control') to run a Silivri story rather like the post-1980 coup Mamak propaganda.[29] A news report, drawn up by a builder perhaps, referring to our cells by the square meterage, and stating, 'There's no question of isolation.'

22 February 2016, *Bugün*

As if I hadn't already mentioned the duplex layout in my first column. 'Isolation' meant separation from other people. A complaint only decent people could understand.

This item inspired me to write the following, and with a smile too:

> The state occupying itself with my property concerns? Let's hope it bodes well!

Our estate agent must have despatched a friendly administrator to promote our development. As the country enters war, that chap must have entered our villa. He snuck in all the way to the bedroom while I was out. Posed on the bed and all. Obviously said something like, 'Snap a few like I'm in a luxury hotel, mate.'

He waxes lyrical enough to make friends and family turn up saying, 'Wonder why we felt so sorry for you; seems you're in paradise after all!'

I read the report; it reads like a 'cemetery with a sea view':

> Duplex apartment, 25 sq. m on each floor, plus a personal fresh air area of 25 sq. m; spacious kitchen, airy windows, hobby rooms, studios… You'd never want to leave, not that you could if you did. I was scared people would be queuing up as if clambering for a TOKİ[30] housing development, God forbid.

22 February 2016, *Bugün*

It's not like there's lots of land left either; such publicity could only backfire… If only the reporter had bothered to linger a little to chat with the owner of the bed! I had such nice things to tell him.

You see, sir:

This used to be a mulberry orchard. Then someone spotted the potential, such a wonderfully vast, huge plot; it was snapped up by a fan and made into a camp for the opposition.

Some ingrates – never knowing what's good for them! – set themselves on fire in protest, not that anyone cared. Best I explain what this place is like, being an inmate here, and tell it like I was telling number one son:

To be honest, I had no intention of moving. It was the landlord of the development who insisted, 'We're gonna bring you here,' and did what he said. I had to move, willy-nilly.

Management had taken a decision when they were constructing the development, offering buyers of villas here the natural conditions of a hundred years previously.

Quite nostalgic really…

Anything that might harm the body was omitted; no telephone, computer, internet, washing – or dishwashing – machines, oven or iron. A totally natural lifestyle…

Laundry is done by treading in a bowl and washing up is done by rubbing with the fingers. There are three sets of plastic dishes and forks for meals. And a second plastic bowl for all the prizes I received in my time here...

The toilet sports an *alla turca* design.

Room service is impeccable... Young men in navy blue suits wait on you.

Intercom using sewerage pipes.

Fantastic...

The gardens might be devoid of soil and flowers, but they are fitted with jogging tracks: private, and with wall views too... The sky visible overhead is thoughtfully obscured by wire netting to protect you from the fierce summer sun.

Sports hall, doctor, barber, masjid, library, courtroom and hospital, all right there, right on the spot...

All that's missing is people. Following the maxim, 'Man is his worst enemy,' they don't want you to meet people.

There is a curfew at any rate. Which, let's face it, is only to be expected under these circumstances...

Thank God our development is the safest place in the city though... Protected by high walls, cameras everywhere... No burglar could intrude. Not that burglars are taken in anyway.

My neighbours matter to me above all.

They're all educated and well read: academics, judges and prosecutors... One is a governor, for instance, and another a colonel... I do believe high-ranking officials are rewarded with lodgings here. I heard the other day that a police chief who'd captured a great thief was given a duplex villa here.

And such a virtuous neighbourhood too... All the residents are straight-laced. No alcohol, no gambling, no women... So none of those impudent women with their seductive ways, laughing out loud and what have you, girls and boys in the same house, adultery or anything.

Fifteen thousand men with worry beads, all in one place.

And let's come to the most important feature:

All this is free...

Three-course meals three times a day, a loaf of bread, room service, armoured shuttles to the city, watching League TV on the box... All free.

I got the electricity bill last month: TL1.98... [31]

And open to the public too... Anyone who annoys Himself has a lifetime access to all these benefits.

Let's say your contract expires – unlikely, yes – and you have to leave. Don't worry; there is an easy way:

Write a couple of lines, or sign some pointless petition, and that's it.

Take me, for example; by adding a couple more sentences to this column, I can easily stretch my residence here to a lifetime; I could even be reincarnated, return, and be reincarcerated here; it's that simple.

The landlord would never say, 'My son's coming back from

Italy, vacate the apartment' or anything; he'd want us to languish here for ever.

Allow me to offer a caveat after all this praise though:

Get cracking; the place is nearly full… There's very little room left.

But the priority will soon be given to the authors of panegyrics for our development, and those who commission said reports…

Once we're out…

Then it will be their turn…

19

PRISON

MY HOROSCOPE in the paper that caught my eye gave me quite a laugh.

'You'll get along well with your loved one in social settings,' it said. 'Unexpected arrangements *might* come into effect. New groups of friends *could* expand your view on life.'

I went over to the iron door and rose on tiptoe to see these 'new groups of friends'; the only 'unexpected arrangement' was a neighbour escorted to a legal visit…

Erdem is in the cell adjacent to mine; never mind meet in 'social settings', we just don't meet at all. When one of us is on his way to a visit, the other is made to wait so we don't see each other. The warder who extends the loaf of bread from the hand-sized hatch hesitates to return my 'Good morning.'

You're alone when you pace, at mealtimes, at the table.

You're forbidden to go to the sports hall, to the studio or the computer room. All your visit requests are refused with the exception of your solicitor, MPs and first-degree relations.

How dangerous, how terrifying must a news item, an idea, a book or a person be to merit such severe isolation, to be segregated from the world like a plague victim?

Would it be more apt to call this a 'quarantine' rather than 'isolation'?

The world-famous illustrator and cartoonist M. K. Perker drew a cartoon the day after we were banged up. We are in a ward with several career criminals asking us, 'God save you brother! What're you in for?' And we reply, 'Journalism.' The killer-faced convict whispers to his mate, 'Let's not mess with these blokes, chief, they're well 'ard, they are.'

Cartoon by M. K. Perker ©

Sadly, the reality was different: gunmen, police officers, intimidators, gang leaders, wife killers, rapists, journalist beaters, newspaper raiders, burglars and smugglers are all free, and journalists are in isolation in a jail with 'special security measures'.

I was reminded of Jeremy Bentham's Panopticon when I first entered Silivri. Bentham's revolutionary eighteenth-century method of reforming human behaviour, that is, a prison based on visibility, had thrown the old system based on locking up.

The Panopticon had a very simple rationale: a tower in the centre, and a circular prison around it. The cells would have wide double-aspect windows. A light from the tower would illuminate the cells and cast the inmates into silhouette.

Bentham was thus replacing the denial of light with a flooding of light, and trapping the inmates with visibility. The cell was visible, but couldn't see, whereas the tower could see without being seen.

Michel Foucault states in *The Birth of the Prison* that the major effect of the Panopticon was to induce in the inmate a state of conscious and permanent visibility that assures the automatic functioning of power. In this system, who wields that power, that is, who sits in the central tower, is immaterial. Even a random visitor is able to form this subjugating relationship. There no longer is any need for iron bars, locks or chains;

the fear of being observed has taken the dungeon from outside the inmate and locked it up inside him.

All too soon, convinced he is being observed even if there's no one in the central tower, the inmate will sit still like a rabbit caught in the headlights.

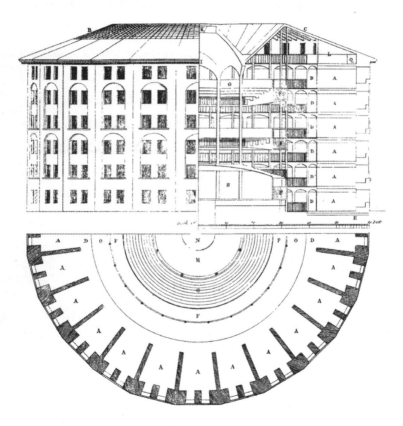

The Panopticon

The Panopticon survives today in high-security prisons equipped with cameras. The camera control room serves as the central tower. Everyone is on edge, aware that he is observed by a huge eye.

The cameras might be unmanned, but the servants' loyalty is unshakeable. As Foucault would say, it is 'the permanent triumph of power without the slightest physical contact…'

Tired of the incessant, illogical and enervating searches in the first few days, I had asked one of the warders, who, instead of replying, snuck a pointing finger at the cameras at either end of the corridor. He meant, 'We're being watched, we have no choice.'

Another, when he was giving me a body search, whispered, 'We're very sorry, but we're seen if we don't search you.' An inmate yelled in the legal visit hall from the other side of a glass partition, 'Careful, there's a camera inside the loudspeaker!' The loudspeaker I'd torn off on my first day, and no one was any the wiser!

Even the belief that there was a camera could force an inmate to be alert for twenty-four hours a day and obey the rules.

That is what a dungeon placed inside the mind creates: a mental siege. The thing to do, therefore, was to refuse to bow down to this surveillance, to pay the 'eye' no heed, and to try to reach an even wider audience. The thing to do was to use all available channels to publish these imprisoned ideas, articles and words whose potential to spread causes such trepidation.

I promised myself that is what I would do. I would turn the arc lamp from the cell to the central tower even if I had to do it all on my own.

20

OUTSIDE

THE DAY after our arrest, Akın came over, bringing news from the outside. He was now my news programme, newspaper, media and bulletin.

He was quite excited as he spoke of the demonstration outside the paper: 'I'd never seen the *Cumhuriyet* like this before! It was raining people!'

The demonstrators marched behind a banner exclaiming, 'IN PURSUIT OF THE TRUTH, WE WON'T BOW DOWN!' The Freedom for Journalists Platform, the International Press Institute and Reporters Without Borders were all there. Secretary General of Reporters Without Borders Christophe Deloire (who in Strasbourg had pleaded with me to stay) had come over from France to make a speech.

Kılıçdaroğlu also took the podium and said, 'A great

journalistic feat by the *Cumhuriyet*: publishing what everyone else was too afraid to publish. Confronting the state was an enormous show of courage.' He then remarked, 'So powerful is this news report that it has resounded. It's the first time there is such public reaction both in Turkey and around the world.'

Demirtaş, for his part, stated, 'We're proud of their upright stance in the face of their arrest.'

PEN International called for our immediate release, describing the arrest order as an outrage.

The International Press Institute expressed their admiration for our 'courageous stand', and the British National Union of Journalists and the American National Press Club also voiced their reaction.

The petition at Change.org was heavily subscribed. Initiated by the Turkish Journalists' Association (TGC) and Reporters Without Borders, it attracted 10,000 signatures on the first day, including such names as Noam Chomsky, Günter Wallraff, Mikis Theodorakis and Claudia Roth.

The European Green Party started a *#FREECANDUNDAR* campaign.

This was all good news.

'What about the press?' I asked.

'Huge reaction in the international press. And here, fifty articles in two days. Even the pool media's ashamed.'

On his way to an EU meeting, Davutoğlu told the members of press flying with him, 'Revealing state secrets is a crime, but trial without detention would be the norm.'

The Italian Prime Minister Renzi stated he was carrying my letter on his way to the meeting. Result? 'Our matter' was discussed behind closed doors, and silence reigned outside. Aslı Aydıntaşbaş summarised the negotiations under her headline 'We offered Can and got the 3 billion.'

Europe – just as I had predicted – had offered Turkey permission for tyranny and money in exchange for stemming the tide of refugees. Instead of speaking, they had grumbled.

'We are troubled,' started the State Department spokesperson, indicating the USA was taking a clearer position. In the meanwhile, the Russian Deputy Minister of Defence claimed, 'They're arrested for having exposed Erdoğan's lie.'

'Has all that hullaballoo helped the paper at least?'

'And how! Treasury inspectors are at the gates already… They've started inspecting the accounts they'd audited previously.'

'Sales?'

'An increase of about 20,000.'

'Oh, well…'

'This is when we're at our strongest. We're not going to bow down,' said Akın, signalling the first clue into our defence:

'We're going to petition the Constitutional Court as individuals. We will also challenge the jurisdiction of the criminal courts … since they're directly under palace control. Your probability of release would be zero. We want to employ a political defence for a political case. We're considering making a stand against this injustice instead of writing long-winded grounds for defence.'

'How do you mean?'

'Our application consists of three sentences: we are doing our duty and, as such, we object to the arrest orders that contradict the Constitution, laws, the European Convention on Human Rights and European Court of Human Rights orders. The rest is up to you. It is your choice, and your responsibility.'

It sounded more like a revolutionary manifesto than the text of an appeal.

I loved it.

There was no need to lose time by playing at extras in this

game of 'courts'. We were going to take a political position at the criminal courts, not a legal one.

I had wholeheartedly approved of this attitude that later attracted such criticism. Might didn't always make you right, but being right always made you mighty. We would derive our might from being right, and walk on, resolute, courageous.

I returned to the cell, happy that we had such a great defence team. Friendly greetings rose from the screen showing the Golden Butterfly Award Ceremony, greetings from such luminaries as Sedat Ergin, Doğan Şentürk, Gülben Ergen and Volkan Konak …

The next morning, I woke up to an İsmail Küçükkaya song: 'Return my greeting, greet the morning.'

When I stepped out into the yard, the sky looked closer and the morning brighter.

21
YARD

THE INNER VOICE OF PACING

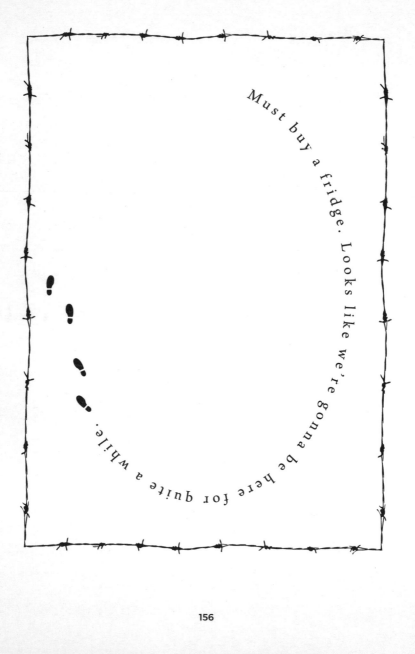

Must buy a fridge. Looks like we're gonna be here for quite a while.

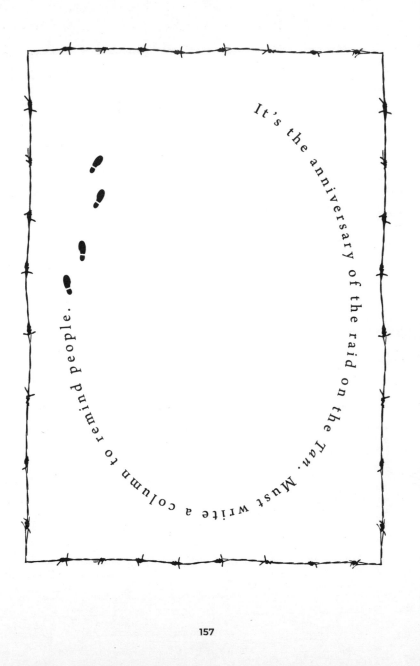

It's the anniversary of the raid on the Tan. Must write a column to remind people.

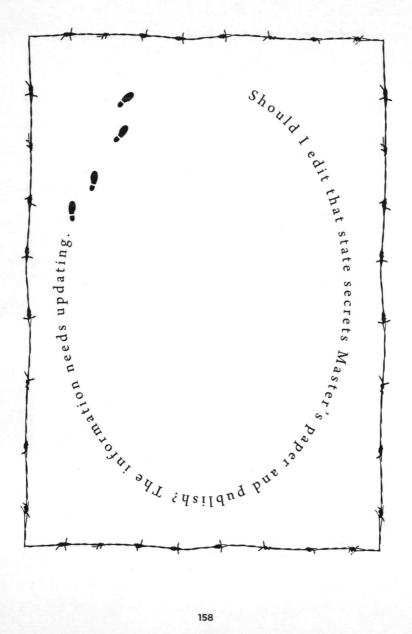

Should I edit that state secrets Master's paper and publish? The information needs updating.

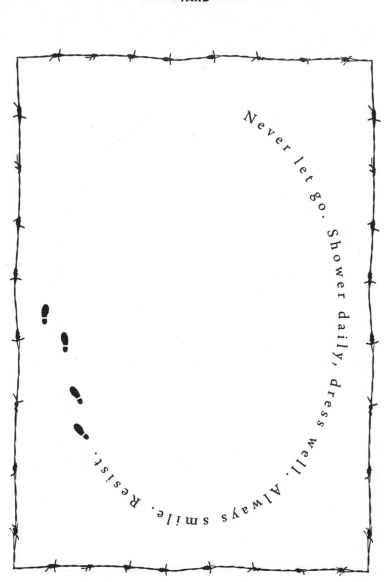

Never let go. Shower daily, dress well. Always smile. Resist.

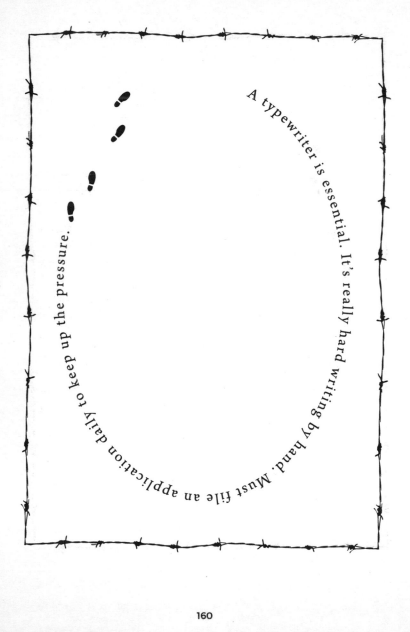

A typewriter is essential. It's really hard writing by hand. Must file an application daily to keep up the pressure.

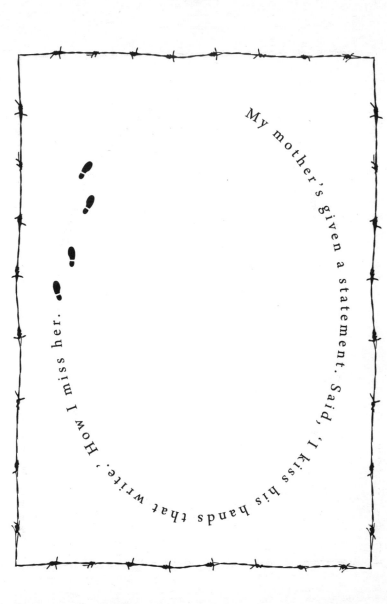

My mother's given a statement. Said, 'I kiss his hands that write.' How I miss her.

Start writing for the world press. It's hard to make yourself heard inside. Must make myself heard to the world.

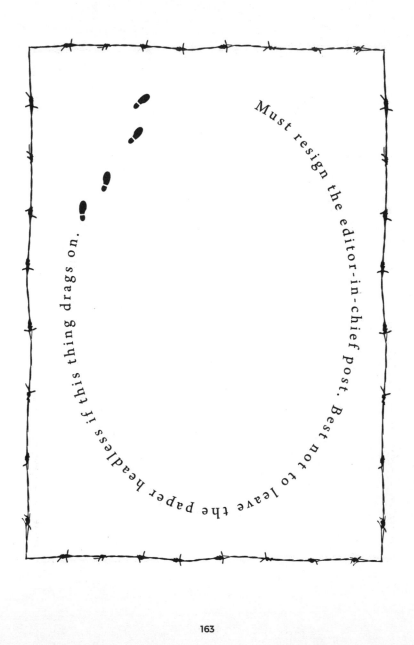

Must resign the editor-in-chief post. Best not to leave the paper headless if this thing drags on.

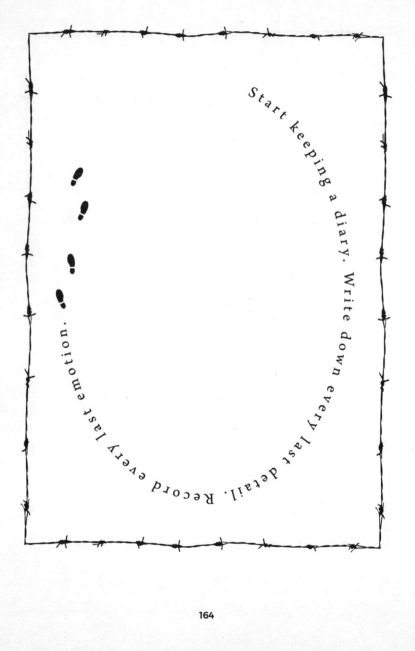

Start keeping a diary. Write down every last detail. Record every last emotion.

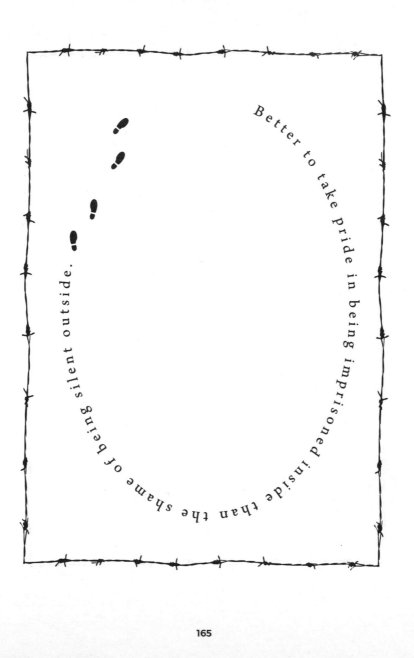

Better to take pride in being imprisoned inside than the shame of being silent outside.

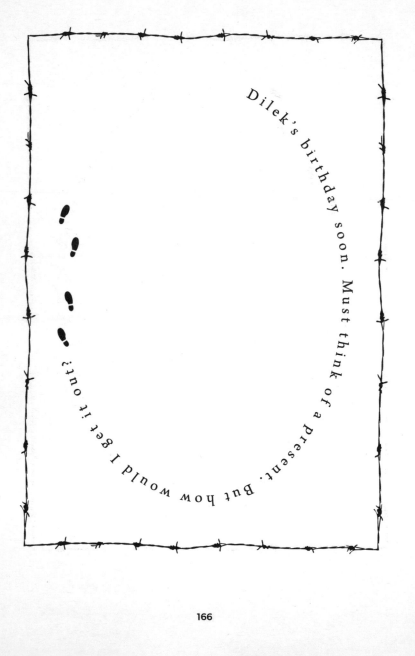

Dilek's birthday soon. Must think of a present. But how would I get it out?

Their objective is to bang us up to browbeat those outside. That's why it's crucial to be even braver.

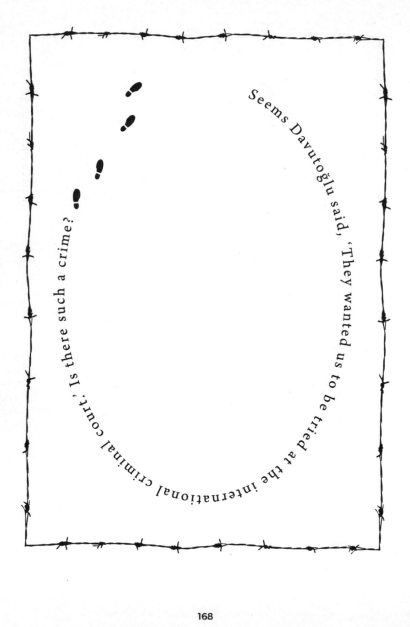

Seems Davutoğlu said, 'They wanted us to be tried at the international criminal court.' Is there such a crime?

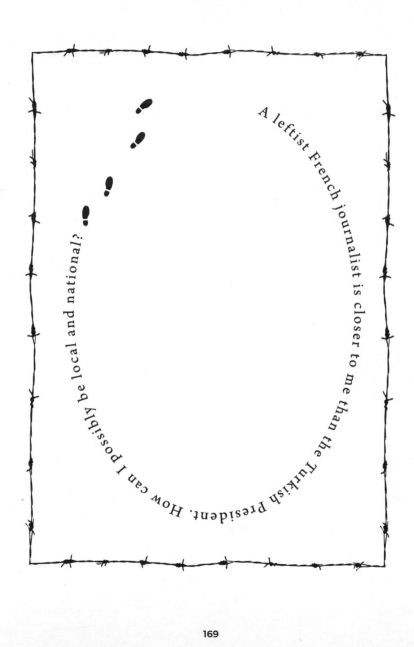

A leftist French journalist is closer to me than the Turkish president. How can I possibly be local and national?

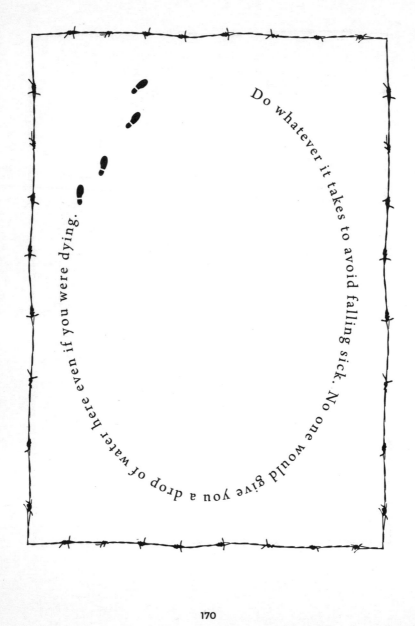

Do whatever it takes to avoid falling sick. No one would give you a drop of water here even if you were dying.

Work like a one-man PR company. Use whatever means you can to send messages.

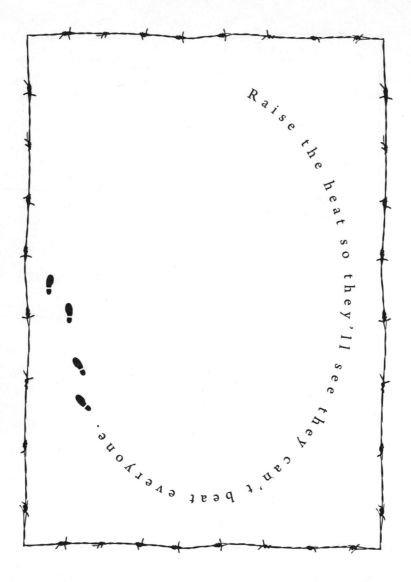

Raise the heat so they'll see they can't beat everyone.

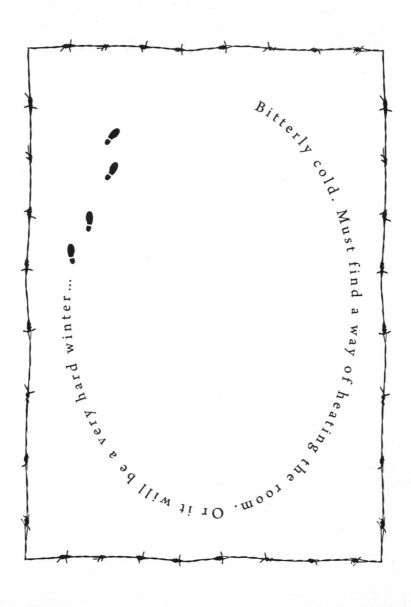

Bitterly cold. Must find a way of heating the room. Or it will be a very hard winter...

22

SISYPHUS

IT'S NOT that the cell is badly heated. The issue is the two-inch gap under the bathroom door. The cold seeps in through there, along with the stench of sewage, turning the ground floor into a bitterly cold loo.

Silivri's troubles are heard by petition. You have to convey every single request in writing. I wrote and despatched mine. They sent me a plasterer. A philosophical young man from Diyarbakır. My first guest in the cell after thirteen days. He drank the tea I made him. I chatted, he talked. The luxury of freedom from a camera. As we chatted, he mixed his mortar, which he poured into a two-inch mould at the bottom of the door. He also located and fixed the dislodged pipe that was the cause of the stench. Then he left.

Waiting for the cement to set into a draught excluder, I was tempted to write something on it – a habit from childhood.

I'd have written *Özgürlük*, but changed my mind, thinking it would be rubbed out. So I wrote it in English instead, hoping they wouldn't get it, and leave it alone.

So you see, on the draught excluder at the bottom of the loo door in cell number 5, corridor A-1, Section 9 of Silivri, it now says 'Freedom'. It is our duty to raise that word up from the floor.

That took the edge off the cold a little, and the smell has abated too. But there still is a half-inch gap. Which I stuffed with – no offence – pool media papers; it did the trick.

All the same, it's cold sleeping downstairs…

I sleep with my feet at the radiator end. The feet are warm, but the head suffers the Siberian cold.

Just then I heard Nedim Şener on a TV debate: the 'old lag' guest was offering advice on keeping warm in prison, as one who'd trod the boards himself.

'Fill a one-litre water bottle with boiling water and place it at your feet when you go to bed,' he said.

Great idea; I tried it straightaway. As my feet were at the radiator end, I cuddled the Goldie brand water bottle as you would a teddy bear. Cuddling my hot Goldie, the bubbly beauty in my bed, I laughed at myself of course. Laughed out loud.

In the meantime, I began reading Nedim's Silivri memoirs, hoping for more advice. The more I read, the more I couldn't believe my eyes.

Nedim had already written the diary[32] I was planning on writing. Down to the last sentence and line.

As I turned the pages, I was astonished when I realised that this new film was pinched from an older one. How could history repeat itself so? Could the god of oppression cheat this much?

Nedim had been arrested in relation to Ergenekon five years ago. He could have been talking of our hearing: 'When we were led back into the chamber, the judge – without even waiting for us to take our place – pronounced the detention order with a brusque, "You may leave." I was sure the decision on us had been made long before the hearing.'

When we had been arrested, the Prime Minister had said, 'They're not arrested for journalism.' It seems Nedim's arrest five years earlier had elicited the same sentence. You'd have thought they'd paraphrase a little at least.

Professional associations had marched and the EU condemned Nedim's arrest at the time. His friends and family all said, 'Thankfully you're here. You'd have been in great danger outside.'

You are allowed visits from three persons outside of family. I named three friends: Tayfun Atay, Tahir Özyurtseven and Murat Sabuncu.

Murat, it turned out, was also Nedim's extra visitor. He repeated what he'd told Nedim: 'The government's uncomfortable with the state of affairs.' I exchanged messages with Nedim: 'Is Murat winding us up or something?'

The night I read Nedim's Silivri memoirs, I was reminded of the legend of Sisyphus. He had defied the gods. His punishment was great enough to match his sin: he was condemned to roll a gigantic boulder up a steep hill. The boulder had to reach the top before daybreak.

He rolled it up all night long. By daybreak, he had reached the top, exhausted, panting. But the gods' hands awaited him there. With a single flick, they rolled the boulder right back down the hill... The punishment that should have been over was beginning again.

Sisyphus would roll the boulder up every night, all the way to the top, and repeat it all over again as soon as day broke.

Now it's our turn to roll the boulder up.

Our crime is the pursuit of truth; it is exposing theft, corruption and lies... Hence the fury of those on the throne... As we suffer our punishment, we try to move that gigantic boulder called 'truth', filled with belief, resolve and endurance, move it into the light. Then the keepers of the night flick the truth back into the darkness with a single move... postponing the light once again. And we, we take over the watch and carry on this endless curse... Waiting for the sleepers to claim the morning one day.

But hold on!

I've not told you about the end of the book yet! Nedim Şener was released, more prestigious than ever before.

'The police inspector behind our arrest,' in his words, is now languishing a few cells away from me. The prosecutor who had issued his arrest warrant has long ago fled abroad. History has a justice system even if mythological gods do not. As İlhan Selçuk says, 'We all carve our own statue in our life-time.' What that statue looks like is up to history to decide.

It was a Yaşar Kemal quote that had helped Nedim clutch on to life. So I cut it out and stuck it at my bedside. That's what our doyen says:

> There's no need for despair at this temporary state of affairs.
>
> Humankind forges hope out of despair.
>
> Democracy or nothing…
>
> Turkey does not deserve 'nothing'.
>
> Greetings, those who confront fear…
>
> Greetings, those who show hope never ends so long as humankind survives…

23

VIGIL

THERE WAS a flood of visitors in the first week, although the Ministry only admitted MPs and solicitors. Even that, however, was enough to stave off the solitude. I am grateful for all the friends, bar associations, MPs and solicitors who rushed over. The mighty embrace of solidarity they offered made us feel at home – and not in the nick.

CHP MPs, in particular, visited as though they were going to work; they came, held our hands, and gave strength, support and hope. They brought news from abroad, from Turkey and from the party. As though we were in the Parliament lobby instead of in Silivri. Political chats renewed our fortitude.

But there is an observation I'd like to share:

Some visitors – solicitors in particular – came as though they were on a condolence visit. Quite possibly expecting me to appear dejected, sad and dispirited, they turned up suitably sombre, and were instead astonished to find me, in total contrast, even more convinced, resilient and in good spirits. The conversation then continued along the lines of us consoling them. I must confess this became a little enervating after a while. The hard thing wasn't consoling them, but confronting the wave of despair outside when I was trying to nurture hope inside. This virus of dejection infecting letters too seemed to have spread far and wide with our arrest, and turned into an epidemic that had knocked the public down.

Sad looks accompanying 'Unfortunately there's nothing we can do's had to be bolstered up with a 'Don't worry, resist; that's what we're doing. We're not losing heart, why should you?'

Sadness was a human emotion, true, but it was only through developing creative reaction methods, organising civil resistance to oppression and making the government regret their injustice that we, and the nation, could attain freedom.

Challenging the ban on a news item, for instance… Defying censorship to delve even deeper and research even more thoroughly would delight us and frighten the government. It would have been wonderful to publish a *Silivri Herald* that gave banned pens an opportunity and published otherwise censored articles. Translating the accused articles into the most widely spoken languages so that the world media could read them would have become a highly effective type of activity.

As I was thinking all this, one of our most respected colleagues arrived at the Silivri gate at 8.30 a.m. on 2 December, carrying a wooden chair on that cold morning. He placed it on the ground. He sat down and started the Vigil of Hope that gave us succour throughout our incarceration.

Columnist Mete Akyol and I had chatted many a time in the past on several documentaries. He was a living history book. He had witnessed countless important events at first hand.

Mete Akyol on his Vigil of Hope

Later, when I testified at the Ergenekon trials, he and I had chatted beyond the wires, talking of our longing for justice.

On that day, when he came for his vigil, he had said, 'I'll stay here for a day. If every colleague keeps this vigil for one day, this could turn into a chain. Today I'm providing the first link in this chain. If another colleague keeps the second, there's the second link.'

And did they make the chain!

I learnt about the protest from the *Cumhuriyet* news item the following day and leapt up, thrilled.

Mete's one-man activity found support straightaway. The Press Council organised the vigil as applicants were put in a queue. Journalist Doğan Satmış arrived on the next day. He was followed by my dear 'sister' Nükhet İpekçi[33] (who said, 'I could be here for my own brother') and the cinematographer Günel Cantak. On the weekend, several organisations arrived bearing banners.

Every new arrival sent greetings through a solicitor, who then carried our voice outside, which is how this mutual support grew. Coach loads came over from a number of counties around the land as the gate hosted folk songs ringing out, award ceremonies, kite festivals and concerts. The 95-year-old architect and writer Aydın Boysan closed a 100-year-old bracket: 'Vahideddin was still on the throne when I was born. Today I feel hesitant; were we freer then?'

Aydın Boysan on vigil

They stood against the mercenary guards of *Ak Saray*, the White Palace: the volunteer guards of Our Palace. In the coldest days of winter, in snow or mud, they carried hope to Silivri in floods. Even when their tiny tent at the gate was demolished ('Forbidden!') 300 people stood on watch close to 1,000 hours. Hundreds more queued enthusiastically.

They filled us with hope day in, day out. We got their messages, heard their voices and held the warm hand of solidarity.

To them we owe gratitude. And to Mete Akyol above all.

Sometimes all it took to defy a gilded throne in the palace was a wooden chair at the prison gate. A tiny tent could defy an enormous palace.

That was made clear.

Mete gave us that chair as a present, and we handed it over to the Press Museum.

So it would never be forgotten...

24

AGENT

ONE OF the hundreds of minutiae that astonish me in prison is this: nothing smells in Silivri.

The campus is so thoroughly surrounded by concrete, iron, wall and mortar that not even odours can penetrate. Neither food, nor soil, flowers, sweat or perfume… (Not counting the sewage.) It was as if the nose were clamped, as if all manners of smell penetration were halted until further notice…

It was in one of the early weeks when a letter breached this blockade and that scent rose up like incense. The enclosed note bore a creative surprise: 'I thought this scent would suit you: Agent Provocateur.'

That drop of black humour served as the only scent in the cell for days.

On the other hand, the pool media adopted the 'agent'

reference quite seriously. The mindset that equates journalism with a job in the public sector agreed with the allegations of 'espionage' on grounds that we had damaged national security. Some members of the pool media tried to nickname me as the Turkish Assange, saying, 'This is a crime even in America.'

I had summarised my attitude on this subject earlier, in the statement I'd given to the prosecutor. But a more solid expression came from the US Ambassador.

8 December 2015, *Cumhuriyet*

Ambassador John Bass made a special point of broaching this point on his visit to the *Cumhuriyet*:

'We are accused of inconsistency and hypocrisy for continuing to press charges against Edward Snowden for disclosing secret documents, yet we support a newspaper for having taken this editorial decision.'

His explanation of this apparent contradiction was utterly consistent: 'True, we do pursue Mr Snowden for breaking US law. But we have not prosecuted American journalists who published the sensitive information he had leaked.'

Touché.

The state tries to conceal its dirty secrets. The press are duty bound to expose them. And if they are exposed, it's not the writer, but the whistle-blower who is charged. If there is a crime in the secret, the guilty party is prosecuted.

Yet, in an effort to live down the crime in the secret, Turkey was trying to turn into a secret the crime exposed by the media.

That week was the seventieth anniversary of the raid on the Tan Press.

In late 1945, a mob was whipped up into a frenzy just when the nation was on the verge of democracy; chanting 'Down with Communists!', they had raided and looted the Tan Press and attacked the staff. None of the attackers was arrested, but Sabiha and Zekeriya Sertel, publishers of the *Tan*, were.

I read their defence[34] while I was inside. This is what Zekeriya Sertel says:

> They riffled through and all they could find amongst my writing was twenty articles. [...] What about the allegation that the Sertels were Russian agents? Shouldn't the government

have utilised all their apparatuses to gather a mountain of documents against us, and [...] using these documents as evidence, prosecute us as Russian agents? [...] Despite all their efforts [...] they found no documentary evidence. All this goes on to show that the real objective is [...] to intimidate other newspapers, to stifle the press and opposition and silence criticism by torturing us. This objective has been achieved.

You can imagine my feelings at reading this defence on its seventieth anniversary. I was accused of being an agent; yet, in the absence of any evidence, I was arrested, charged with fifty-two of my articles.

You know how serious offenders are taken into therapy and asked to speak of their childhood? If we were to ask our seventy-year-old democracy – that has form! – to speak of its childhood, the first thing it will mention is the *Tan* affair.

The breech birth of seventy years ago smothered freedom in the cradle and raised a democracy without a left arm.

It is that dark history that empowers the guilty and their crimes.

25

WORLD

THE GREAT and the good who rule us want us to be 'local and national'. Anyone voicing this oppression abroad is branded a snitch. Which means: 'We'll beat you, and you'll take it like a man! All this oppression is for the good of the country…'

Yet the leftist tradition that raised me views the love of country as not an obstacle to, but a support for an international solidarity that transcends boundaries. It's not countries that connect people but their principles: Freedom, democracy, human rights, secularity and justice…

Where they are absent, that land could never be our 'country'.

Solidarity with the family of humankind helps us free the land where we live from domestic despots and join the free world. We are connected by ideas, conscience and class;

ties of considered judgement, not genetic or congenital characteristics like race, colour or nationality.

For example, Fehmi Tosun, a Kurdish family man, was kidnapped by a white Renault Toros, the standard plain-clothesmen's vehicle, in 1995, never to be seen again. Fifteen years later, U2 gave a concert in Istanbul on 6 September 2010, and Bono sang 'Mothers of the Disappeared' for Tosun: 'In the wind we hear their laughter / In the rain we see their tears / Hear their heartbeat, we hear their heartbeat.'

The white Toros and the murderer inside were local and national. But we don't like our compatriot the murderer. We like our comrade Bono. What connects us is not blood but life.

Country, I hear?

The place forfeited to the thieves, fiends and murderers? The place we've risked prison for – to liberate it from those thieves, fiends and murderers? Our captive land whose streams, coasts and forests we're killing ourselves to save from the plunderers?

We never ravaged but revered it instead.

Although most of us had the opportunity to live in comfort somewhere else in the world, the thought never even crossed our minds; we stayed here. We fought for the future of our country, of our generation and those coming after us. We put our heart and soul into our work, saying, 'We love our country, but what really matters is for our country to love us.'

And when we were captured in return, we dug tunnels out to the free world from our 'local' dungeon.

Throughout our time in Silivri, I grew to appreciate the value of global solidarity the more the 'nationalist' press under the plunderer's thumb sided with the oppressor and the quieter the centrist media fell – lest they be next.

And I called out to the freedom-loving family of humankind.

In the first week, I founded a public relations office whose entire inventory consisted of a plastic desk, a plastic chair, a pen and a wad of paper.

I started writing. I tried to make my voice heard with a letter, column, statement or message to every single visitor, every demonstration and every newspaper. I was like an accident victim who was desperate to be heard from the bottom of the well he'd fallen into. Whatever I wrote was taken out either by solicitors or MP friends.

Dilek and Ege were working like the external troopers of my one-man office, running from one country to the next to contact press organisations. Pınar Ersoy and Berivan Aydın, our two foreign press angels at the *Cumhuriyet*, were translating and conveying to the world at large whatever I sent out.

Friends everywhere were using these messages to point out the danger facing Turkey: Reporters Without Borders, Faruk Günaltay and Ahmet İnsel in France, Nilgün Cerrahoğlu and Ceyda Karan in Italy, Semra Uzun-Önder in Germany, Şule

Bucak in the UK and CHP MPs and others at the European Parliament (led by Utku Çakırözer and Gülsün Bilgehan).

Other inmates might be working on their defences with their solicitors; our meetings went more like this:

'Have you written to the *Washington Post*? And *Der Spiegel* is waiting for an article. The one you sent to *The Guardian* was published yesterday. France is important. You must write to *Le Monde*. You must send a message to the ceremony in Strasbourg. The AP are working on a report; you must reach that researcher.'

Thanks to this mobilisation, it didn't take long before the world began to hear our voices – by the second week, in fact.

On 2 December, German Greens started a campaign to have us freed.

On 4 December, banners were opened outside the WDR building in Cologne.

8 December 2015, *Cumhuriyet*

On 5 December, a motion was passed calling for our release at the House of Commons.

On 7 December, a support demonstration took place outside the White House.

On 10 December, Dilek and Ege received the City Honour Medal conferred by the Strasbourg council.

Dilek later attended the PEN Netherlands Freedom of Speech ceremony.

Dilek shuttled between capitals like Washington, Berlin, Stockholm and
Paris like a Foreign Secretary determined to secure our release.

On 12 December, the German Social Democrat Party Congress
adopted a motion calling for our release.

That same evening, the *Libération* organised a solidarity
event for us in Paris.

Visiting my office at the paper, George Papandreou, the
President of Socialist International, issued a message of
support.

World-famous comrades joined in this mobilisation.

Fazıl Say mentioned us in his concerts abroad as Orhan
Pamuk spoke of us in interviews.

Cinematographers Canberk Benli and Günel Cantak
told the story of our imprisonment in a short video in four

languages: *#WeAreArrested* soon reached all corners of the globe.

On 12 December, Murat Sabuncu's inspired idea brought the *Cumhuriyet* news meeting to the Silivri gate. My colleagues with whom I pursued news day in, day out, debated the agenda in their coats. Then Tahir came 'inside' for a visit and asked me for the headline.

16 December 2015

The first thing that popped into my head was 'Yet Another First in Turkey'.

We could easily have said '…the World'.

This symbolic action, holding a news meeting outside the greatest journalist prison in the world, was widely reported on prestigious TV channels around the world. It was a huge boost to morale to see that the messages rolled into bottles and sent out by the 'lonely man inside' did actually touch some hearts outside. This mobilisation climaxed in mid-January.

Dilek said, 'Got a call from the US Embassy on the way. Joe Biden wants to meet me,' when she arrived for a closed visit. It was a highly telling gesture for the US Vice-President to ask to meet the family of a journalist imprisoned on the basis of Erdoğan's complaint before *their* meeting. We agreed that Ege should also attend.

I was to learn later that Ege's International Relations course in London had scheduled an exam on American foreign policy that week. In a twist of fate, he had to ask for leave on grounds of 'having a meeting with the US Vice-President' so he could come to Istanbul.

I watched Dilek and Ege emerge from their meeting with Biden on my TV.

Ege told the cameras: 'It was a brief meeting. He called my father very brave. "You must be proud of him," he said.'

I learnt more of the detail at our next visit.

Biden had said that the US warnings on freedom of the press would continue, and reminded them of Thomas Jefferson's words: 'Were it left to me to decide whether we should have a government without newspapers, or newspapers without a government, I should not hesitate a moment to prefer the latter.'

Ege and Dilek Dündar after their meeting
with Biden, 22 January 2016

That the US had lost faith in Erdoğan was obvious. That's what this meeting had signalled. It was, needless to say, quite a surprising message for those of us who had grown up with the slogan 'Down with American imperialism!'

This international solidarity bolstered up my resistance in prison. It was as if a familiar song rang out in the cell: 'I hear your heartbeat,' it said.

Our hearts beat even more joyfully.

26

LETTER

DO YOU recall the name James Gregory?

Sergeant Gregory was Mandela's racist warder. His command of Madiba's mother tongue had put him in charge of the imprisoned ANC leader's communications and of censoring his letters in the top prison of South Africa.

At first, Gregory is convinced that 'terrorist Mandela' should be hanged, but his views change as he gets to know the man. When, twenty-seven years later, Mandela is at last freed and elected South Africa's first black President, Gregory stands beside him.

I watched *Goodbye Bafana*, the film based on Sgt Gregory's account, on Silivri TV. This was channel 29 on our 29-channel TV sets. All day long it broadcast the list of products available in the canteen, and then, at 9 p.m., it ran a good film on DVD.

You may well ask, 'What's so great about showing prisoners a prison movie?' You will have to appreciate, however, that the tale of a lifer's rise to President shone a matchless ray of hope from the colourful box to that drab cell.

The really interesting point for me, though, was Gregory's growing respect for his charge. Our own 'letter man' popped into mind unbidden. Was he also impressed by my letters?

I must tell you about our 'letter man'.

This baby-faced young warder works on the Silivri Letter Reading Commission. We hand him every letter we write, folded into an unsealed, stamped envelope. He reads it all, stamps 'Checked' on a blank corner if there's nothing 'objectionable' in it, seals the envelope and posts the letter.

He also opens every letter that we receive, removes any 'objectionable' enclosures (such as dried flowers, leaves etc.), reads it and stamps 'Checked', again, on a corner, and hands it out. We hand over our letters on Mondays, Tuesdays and Thursdays at morning roll call, and receive ours on Wednesdays and Fridays.

I had put my address at the bottom of one of the first articles I'd sent in with the note, 'You might not have written a letter for quite a while.' I received hundreds of letters afterwards, a number that only increased from week to week. I now couldn't wait for Wednesday and Friday afternoons for the post to come.

True, envelopes slit on one side might have taken the edge off the joy of opening a letter, but they also blessed the cell with passion, a throwback to a past century.

I laid all the letters out on my desk, separated those bearing familiar signatures, put them all in order, and then savoured reading them one by one.

It was so different from email.

Firstly, no one wrote to curse or sound off; instead, everyone offered sincere support and watered love lest I might dry up inside. Virtually every single one was handwritten on a vast variety of paper. The ruled sheets ripped out of bound notebooks still bore the warmth of young readers.

These were lines that didn't necessarily expect a reply; they comforted and cheered me up.

Most shared an opening sentence: 'I'd not written to anyone for quite a while.' Some were writing a letter for the first time.

Fantastic!

It was like a forgotten friend had returned to my life.

This introduction was usually followed by an apology for the illegible handwriting. Those scrawls spoke of the tremors of pupils who got 'Average' for handwriting, or of hands that had lost the skill to write thanks to computers.

Next…

Next came pessimism, prefaced by, 'I don't know if you'll get this letter…'

Despondent expressions of gloom on the course the country was taking, astonishment at what had happened to us, prophecy that this would only escalate and despair at not knowing what to do. As though they were in prison, and not us. Most were in this vein.

It was as if we were the last generation who trusted the future.

For a while I replied to each and every one with a postcard bearing images of a mosque or a forest (available in the canteen) and invited them all to hope, 'Don't whine, speak. Don't lament, move. Don't murmur, object. Don't whinge, fight. Don't give into woes, resist.'

There was enough grief inside; what we needed was cheering up. They should be giving us a shot in the arm. But pessimism had spread like a contagious disease; it had enslaved hearts and minds. There was no point in shouting, 'Don't lose hope!' from prison. The best thing to do was to spread hope, in the belief that courage was as contagious as despair.

That's what I tried to do.

To be fair, though, countless envelopes revealed colourful cards, smiling photos and floral papers that signalled an anxious effort to supply a still hopeful inmate with ammunition.

Take your pick: blue cruise scenes from people guessing my longing for nature or shots of beautiful women 'animated' with heady scents?

Hopeless inmates who end their letters with, 'I can't afford a second sheet, so have to finish here'?

Friends who enter a post office that's stood ignored on their beaten path for many years, lick a stamp for the first time since childhood, and recall the phrase, 'Signed for?'

The one that made me laugh most was one returned with the phrase, 'Not known at this address.'

Then there was the notice: 'You have a parcel. Come and collect it at the Silivri Post Office.'

I safeguard those letters as the comrades of a hard time, as the confidants and documents of troubled times.

As for our 'letter man'...

His workload increased, naturally, as letters grew ever more numerous through the weeks. There were so many that even I was struggling to read them all; but his job was to read each and every one.

He might have deprived me of the joy of opening my own envelopes, of being the first one to read those wonderful lines, but he had bitten off more than he could chew. He could easily see the interest in the 'spy' charged with two life sentences, and bear witness to the lines full of support and love. It was highly likely that he shared the most important letters with 'the authorities'.

I wonder what he felt as he read them?

Did he get emotional?

Did he wonder, 'X hasn't written in a while; I hope nothing's wrong,' like I did?

Did some letters that made me well up make him cry too?

Did he copy some of the best pages for himself?

Did he read them out to his mates for a laugh?

Was he happy to be the first to sniff the perfume sprayed on lines filled with longing or the first one to hear the notes emanating from musical cards?

When he wanted to write to someone, did he quote/copy our letters?

As I mused over all this, a curious phenomenon arose. Some cheeky friends had begun to greet him in every letter.

Letters now began, 'Dear Can, and the Fella Reading his Letters,' and one even enclosed a second letter, specifically addressed to him: 'Your job's really tough. Is it very tiring? Are you sick of reading all those letters? Look after Can well.'

Needless to say, the warder didn't keep those lines for himself; he made sure I got them all. I had great fun reading them, but did they wind him up?

I would peer inquisitively at his face at every letter delivery time, looking for the slightest hint.

Imagine coming face to face with the man who bugs your telephone: we met in the written version of this scenario. He knew me down to the last line, but I didn't even know his name.

He was quite phlegmatic, of the type that would be called

poker-faced in English. He might be a diligent intelligence man, scrutinising every letter in minute detail. Or he might be a lazy penitentiary protection officer who just stamped everything and passed it on.

I let my imagination run wild, weaving stories about him.

He would add his own observations to the letters come the day: 'Best not to trust X quite so much,' 'You've neglected Y for quite a while,' 'This bloke's trying to dig your grave,' or, 'That last letter you wrote your son was really emotional.'

Then we would start writing to each other, and end up as penfriends who communicate daily, but never talk.

We would prove the censorship-defying connection formed by letters.

We would become friends just like Mandela and Gregory.

We would leave this wretched prison and jointly write our memoirs.

Don't dismiss the idea; it has been known. *Checked.*

27
OUT

THE DECEMBER sun is fragile, timid and pale...

It's barely poked its head over the roof for days on end. It floats down over the high wall around the yard, reluctantly like a yellow kite. I keep waiting for it to descend so we can be reunited. But no. It draws back cruelly with only ten feet to go.

Can you leap up to the sun? I try, leap up and reach on tiptoe to touch it; to no avail. It bounds over the wire and hurries away.

All you're left with is the buzzing, sulking official light of the fluorescent all day long...

The first time I left Silivri was for a hearing on the twenty-second day of my incarceration.

I'd been dreaming of a reunion with the sun, of touching it and feeling its warmth on my skin when I was out. But what greeted me instead was the odious countenance of a filthy winter rain. The winter sun that had been frolicking on the roof for days had hidden behind grim clouds the moment I was out.

It was 17 December. And I was on my way to answer for my 17 December articles on thieves.

It was highly likely that the date was specifically chosen. But I was determined: instead of being called to account for my actions, I was going to ask those who should be called to account for their actions.

I rose early. Had my shower. Got dressed in the outfit that I had been arrested in. Started waiting. Penitentiary protection officers took me out of my cell, conducted a search and handed me over to the gendarmes, who also conducted their own search, took charge, put me in a prisoner transport van and set off.

This wasn't one of those blue transport vehicles with the grille over a tiny window that we frequently see on the roads; this was a vehicle specifically intended for individual prisoners who were not 'organisation members'.

A captain sat in the passenger seat next to the driver in the front and the prisoner was in a secure section behind them in an arrangement essentially little larger than a two-man box that could have been a mobile cage blocked off from the front seats by a glass partition. To the rear, separated by a wire screen, three or four armed gendarme troops sat on watch.

Handcuffing the prisoner was the team commander's call.

I was never handcuffed, nor ever treated with anything other than impeccable courtesy.

I took a look at the young gendarme trooper who was conducting my search. He was the same age as my son. My columns had been probing what would have a bearing on his money, his country, and his future; those were the columns I was presently going to be tried for. 'If only I could tell him that,' I thought to myself.

We boarded the prisoner transport van and set off on the great journey beyond the Great Wall of Oppression.

We joined the motorway by the 'Last Hope Kiosk' where friends were keeping vigil. The tent of hope stood like a modest, yet proud flag. I saw soil for the first time in three weeks. The earth's blanket that I might never miss in the hustle and bustle of everyday life looked like a long-lost relation, albeit still in winter drabs…

The familiar district names on road signs could have been the names of far distant continents…

The city flowing past the windows played behind a wire cage for the first time: in dribs and drabs, in pieces, distant, wet…

Dozens of prisoner transport vans moved in a convoy. Mobile prisons moving between captivity and hope…

And me, in one such van…

I was on my way to the Justice Palace to answer the charge of insulting the incumbent of the Unauthorised Palace.

The loneliness of three weeks stared quizzically at the crowds on the streets: people in a hurry, scudded by a strong wind… High buildings yearning for the bright lights of New Years past… And finally, in Çağlayan, the terminus for pursuers of justice: the palace…

Crowds at the entrance… It seemed the nation had yet to drop the charges against its rulers.

I was overjoyed to hear supporters call out my name as the van drove in.

The mobile prison twisted down and down, as if moving in the bowels of the palace, and entered a noisy prisoner-only world underground. I was in the dungeons of the iceberg called Justice Palace, where I would wait to be taken up to the ground floor to be weighed on the scales of the blindfolded Goddess of Justice.

My gendarme escort and I found ourselves in the midst of a riot: it was bedlam, detainees attacking one another as guards tried to separate them. I was scuttled into a cage. A real cage: a stone room with walls on three sides and iron bars all the way to the ceiling on the fourth. All that was missing was a sign: 'Species: Human, Caution: Please do not throw pens.'

A bashful gendarme commander admitted, 'It's for your own safety; you never can tell with the people here.'

Handcuffed detainees passed by my cage in ones and twos. I locked eyes with every single one. Deflated steps dragged mostly young, exhausted bodies between the gendarmes.

Most were robbers. 'Petty criminals', of course… If they had stolen big, they would have been the judges, not the judged.

Taking a dispassionate look at the drug addicts, tough lads, hard men yelling and fighting and the random 'spy' amongst them, I thought, 'Wouldn't Günter Wallraff[35] die to be here now!'

Then the time came. My cage was opened.

A long corridor connected us to a small lift. The small lift opened out into a big hall. The moment we stepped into the hall, a thunderous applause rose.

A hundred smiling faces in the hall. Warm.

I felt I'd just touched the sun.

My loneliness melted away in a moment…

I warmed up.

Can Dündar with the HDP Istanbul MP Filiz Kerestecioğlu,

19 February 2016

I returned to Silivri with my heart at peace, having said what I needed to say in court, and having seen the people I wanted to see at the hearing.

In the same transport van.

Where the real criminals ought to have been.

I was tired.

I noticed how my body had grown stiff after three weeks of indolence, how quickly the muscles gave out. I turned in early.

In the middle of the night, I was awakened by shouts. It was unusual in the dark silence of Silivri. I opened the window, curious, and listened out.

Someone was yelling, 'Thief! Watch your stuff!' Someone was being burgled, I thought; so he was yelling to alert the others, and the warning passed along from cell to cell, ear to ear. I followed suit and yelled.

My shout, 'Thief!' echoed from the walls.

The announcement rose up into the skies. Then I suddenly recalled the date.

It was 17 December. That's when the reason for the shouts sank in.

In ordinary countries the police catch the thieves; here, the thieves had had their police caught.

Shout, and you got it.

28

NEW YEAR'S EVE

SNOW.

At the end of December, first we had a bit of sleet, just a drizzle. Then it formed an army of cotton wool that settled in the yard through the night.

It sprinkled confetti from the roofs, dancing in the search-lights.

I watched from the window: the snowflakes shoved and pushed each other all the time. They couldn't stick on the stone though. Just melted and vanished.

We're under curfew at night in Silivri, but the snow is not.

But while we were all asleep, the snowflakes grew aware. Realising they melted when they landed singly on the stones, they got together. They stopped scuffling, united and snowed hard enough to conquer the yard.

When I looked in the morning, I saw that the snow lay in the yard like a spotless sheet. I pulled on my coat and flung myself on top of the snow to leave a Can-shaped mark. Enjoyed the pure white.

Gloves are forbidden. The warder had withheld the red gloves that had been sent by parcel post. So I shook hands with the snow without gloves. I wrote my favourite names in huge letters in the yard so passing aircraft could read them.

I drew shapes with my footsteps and battered the iron gate with snowballs. Just as I was about to make a Can-snowman, a parcel sailed over the wall and fell into the yard.

This time, my neighbour Murat's parcel contained a hot cheese toastie.

But how? The canteen had neither toasties, nor sandwich toasters. I ate what was set before me and asked no questions.

Murat and Cevheri were about to be tried on charges of 'inciting an uprising' over a magazine cover they'd published. I thanked him through the grate and conveyed my wishes that they would be released, 'You'll spend New Year's Eve at home,' I said.

Later, as they left for the court, I heard their footsteps in the corridor. And in the afternoon came the news: they would be released. A last parcel fell into the yard towards evening: another hot cheese toastie. And a note:

Thank you for your prayers. This feels so bittersweet. We
were great neighbours. What's not great is that I'm leaving
without giving you the toastie recipe.

Murat

As I enjoyed my friendly neighbour's toastie, a second parcel arrived: this time it was dark (*bitter* in Turkish!) chocolate
from Cevheri. Spot on, given the circumstances.

We were all prisoners of the same tyranny. Held by the mindset that said, 'The only good journalist is a detained journalist,'
and the fixation with intimidating those outside by locking up
opponents on farcical allegations certain to be thrown out of
court at the first hearing.

What we went through was a holiday compared to the
attacks in the Kurdish districts of Sur, Cizre and Silopi, or the
human tragedy witnessed on the Aegean Sea; except it was
still prison all the same, it was isolation.

The *Nokta* men's footsteps rang through the corridor at
night after the yard doors were locked. They were leaving.

'God save you,' they called out to us who were left behind.

'God save Turkey from this bane,' we replied. Once that was
gone, everyone would be saved anyway.

As the 'Silivri estate agent' was planning new prisoners
for the freed cells, the recipe for the hot toastie appeared in
the *BirGün* of the following day, unsurprisingly from another

old lag. Doğan Tılıç gave the '80s model, Mamak-style recipe in his column: 'Quarter a loaf of bread. Remove the inside and replace with the cheese. Wrap it in a carrier bag, and place it between the radiator columns. Your hot toastie is ready in the morning.'

It was ingenious. Of course I tried it that night. And awoke to the last day of the year with a hot toastie cooked in a radiator fire. Waiting for me in its narrow slot, warmed through to the heart.

If life is the art of finding happiness in small things, prison is an art college…

In his final column of the year, Ertuğrul Özkök was asking for our permission to have fun at New Year's.

Sometimes, just on the eve of the best night, you think of someone accompanying a loved one to an Intensive Care Unit, a prisoner in solitary, a refugee in the middle of the sea, a child getting into bed trembling at the prospect of paternal abuse or a beggar looking forward to the next morning's rich pickings in the bins…

Thoughts to freeze laughter in the mouth and choke the joy in the throat.

And yet, if you are one of the wretches listed above – and on 31 December I most certainly was – you don't want to rain on others' parade either.

You say to yourself, 'I hope my friends aren't too down at heart just because I'm here… On the contrary, I hope they have fun for me too.'

When you're inside, it's only joy that will cure you, not sorrow. Your pain is alleviated through the happiness of your loved ones. Your jailer knows by your laughter that he can't vanquish you.

This is the triumph of life.

In his *Man's Search for Meaning,*[36] Viktor E. Frankl recounts how inmates in Nazi concentration camps who had lost everything resisted the sense of meaninglessness and thereby transformed defeat into triumph.

The book offers a heartbreaking observation on the festive season:

The chief doctor of the camp noticed that the death rate in the week between Christmas 1944 and New Year's Eve increased beyond all previous experience. He did his research.

The working conditions were not harder. The food supplies hadn't deteriorated. The weather hadn't changed. There wasn't a new epidemic.

It was simply that the majority of the prisoners had lived in the naïve hope that they would be home again by Christmas. As the time drew near and there was no encouraging news, the prisoners lost courage and disappointment overcame them.

This had a dangerous influence on their powers of resistance and a great number of them died.[37]

Meaning...

What helps people survive is the determination to live.

That is why Frankl recommends prisoners adopt a Nietzsche quote as a slogan: Those who have a 'why' to live, can bear with almost any 'how'.

I had a 'why' and had stopped fretting over the 'how'...

I'd made a great New Year's Eve plan.

Supper was lentil soup, two chicken drumsticks and vermicelli pastry. I would season the drumsticks with thyme and black pepper, pretend my sour cherry juice in a teacup was wine and slouch in the pyjama-slippers-TV mode. Playing cards sent to me had been seized, so I couldn't play solitaire. Tombola was also out of the question, since I didn't have a quorum.

Instead, I would do a year-end account, given I was on my own.

I would contemplate, 'Where am I in my book of life? How should I summarise the finished chapters? How should I write the remaining pages? Is prison going to be a crossroads? Will my disappointments stick? Will my anger simmer down?'

As it turned out, I didn't do any of this and instead I had the worst New Year's Eve of my life, quite unexpectedly, and for an entirely different reason.

The *Cumhuriyet* had announced that a kite festival would be organised in Silivri at 1 p.m. to cheer us up, and that Dilek and Ege would also participate. But the snowstorm had turned into a massive blizzard.

Ege had got a bee in his bonnet about 'gathering friends to sing outside Silivri at night' and it had taken all my persuasive powers to change his mind. At 12.30 p.m., however, the TV reported a thirty-vehicle pile-up on the way to Silivri and that several people were seriously hurt.

I was hurt. Worried. Concerned.

Bothered – for the first time – by my lack of telephone, lack of communication.

There was no more news. Nothing on any of the channels. No one said anything. I felt helpless.

As worry gnawed at my insides, I started pacing in the cell like a demented man, chewing at my nails. Swore my heart out at those who made me suffer so, to have kept me away from my loved ones on this New Year's Eve – and I had no idea how many more I had in store; cursed those fugitives from the human race to my heart's content.

I was to learn later that the heavy snowfall had cancelled the event, which meant my friends hadn't come. But a mountaineer of the '68 generation had decided to spend the night with us. The 69-year-old Cafer Sungur heaved his tent on his back and came to Silivri gate. Spent the night there. Shouted,

'Happy New Year!' at midnight, hoping we'd hear, but the gendarme on watch stopped him. Realising he ran the risk of freezing before daybreak, he sought shelter in the mosque.

A noble one-man ceremony…

But that night I heard neither the '68er mountaineer's friendly voice, nor, indeed, any news from outside. I thought they'd let me know if there was anything serious.

I cancelled my celebrations.

Cafer Sungur with his tent on the New Year's Eve Vigil of Hope

I decided to bury myself in books to dispel any negative thoughts. Işık Öğütçü had sent me Orhan Kemal's biography; I read that until midnight. I called out at Erdem's cell after supper, 'Happy New Year!' and was delighted at receiving a reply.

At midnight, I watched a Coldplay concert on Bloomberg, followed by a Victoria's Secret show. I felt better at the thought that Victoria's secrets were finer than those of our intelligence agency's.

I wished a free year to my possessions in the cell as Turkey counted down from ten. I wrote two letters in the first couple of hours of the new year. The first to myself, and the second to Ege.

Dear Me,

I believe this might well be the first New Year's Eve when you and I are together, on our own, unaccompanied by crowds gathered to dispel the thoughts of years flashing past and laughter concealing inner boredom.

I am aware that you, the top of my list of neglected loved ones, deserved a much earlier, much longer, and much more detailed chat and kindness that prioritised you.

I owe you an apology for delaying this for so long, and thanks to those who have brought us together here.

Don't you agree that this is the ideal environment to make up for lost time and a perfect evening?

Shall we sit up all night, chatting to get to understand each other better, to remember our past and plan our future?

After finishing this note, we spoke with him for a while… We had a bit of a reckoning. We took some serious decisions that I carved into my mind, witnessed by the walls, but would never consider writing down here. I didn't string it out. 2 January was Ege's birthday. I'd planned to congratulate him with a column in the paper. I wrote it before daybreak.

A SMALL, FLAT STONE

Closed visit day…

I ran over to the visit room.

A slim twenty-year-old in the narrow cabin behind the glass…

My son…

His arms burgeoning, fingers touching that thick pane of glass between us.

Our palms meet on either side.

'Meet' is just a turn of phrase here.

Pane between two pals.

There had been mountains, oceans, and continents between us before, but never had we been so close and yet so far, too far to touch.

Now that we're close enough to touch, we're going to talk on the phone as if there were continents between us.

Our eyes will do what our hands cannot; we'll touch with our gaze.

It's his birthday today.

He's twenty now.

Two inseparable decades…

The cold pane between us now trying to drive a wedge between us.

I'd written, 'Dear friends, we're going to have a son,' the week he was due.

Sezen was singing, 'My Heart's Still in the Aegean' just then.

His mother and I agreed on Ege.

In our home that is a temple to smiles, we witnessed his first word, first steps, first love.

Books were his favourite toys.

He grew up writing.

Dilek would be judging panel and we would hold writing competitions at home:

Describe a smell in words.

I would describe thyme, and he, mint.

We would teach our pens to smell.

We'd keep writing until we had co-authored a book of children's stories.

Later, I wrote *The Red Bicycle* for him.

It was about the bike I'd taught him to ride; how I let go of the back and how he sped away, secure in his belief that I was still holding on ...

And how I gazed behind him, approving.

Two decades of never hurting each other.

Neither a single toddler tantrum, nor an adolescent's moods.

On Mother's Day, I wrote the lyrics and he composed the song we sang to wake her up.

On Father's Day we picked the flattest stones to skip on the water in Eymir.

We cried by the bed where we'd lost his grandpa.

We laughed when our story was staged as a children's play.

That carefully planted sapling shot up; the more I wound him up ('You'll never be as tall as me!') the taller he grew. Now he stands head and shoulders above me. My baby I used to cuddle blessed me with the unique joy of resting my head on his chest now.

We raised each other.

One evening recently, I sat on the plastic chair in some desolate cell and watched him in the lighted box facing me.

It used to be the other way round.

When he was a child, every time I was on TV, he used to go round the back and look for me inside that lighted box.

And now, he was in the box that for years I'd spoken out of as he listened.

He was talking of justice, freedom and oppression with greater maturity than would be expected of someone his age.

I wanted to go behind the box and give him a huge hug.

Then he wrote for the *Cumhuriyet*.

The pen that had drawn my life was now pouring forth, cascading between his fingers.

The topic was no longer thyme and mint; now it was freedom and justice.

On the day that my son turned up beside me, I cried buckets, just as I had done on the day my father had flown away.

As I did on that visit day when he showed me the little flat stone he'd snuck in his pocket.

The moment he'd turned into a distant lake beyond the cold glass.

Listening ears would have noted:

Neither did I ask him, 'Have you zeroed it all?' nor did he inform me, 'It's all transferred, Daddy.'

We talked of the films and documentaries we'd seen, poems and essays we'd written and books we'd read.

Thankfully we are where we are without ever deceiving or being deceived, without ever having stolen, ever taken a penny that wasn't ours. We are clean.

Today is 2 January.

All I have to give him as a present is this column.

But I'm sure the warmth of two palms on either side of a glass pane will one day take its place in a poem, a biography or a book as a distant, sad memory.

And he and I will be driving an open-top towards the

horizon on some continent far away as we've always dreamt of.

Our wonderful chat was interrupted by the commanding voice of the penitentiary protection officer saying, 'Time's up.'

The telephone line was cut.

The palms stuck to the glass once again.

The twenty-year-old sapling left.

A proud pair of eyes stared at his back…

My heart's in the Aegean.

29

HOSPITAL

LAST SUMMER I took Tahir's advice and started orthodontic treatment to straighten my crooked lower teeth.

I must confess it took quite a while for me to stop digging my heels in and agree. The idea of wearing braces at this age, going for weekly check-ups in my hectic schedule and putting up with aching jaws all seemed far too much.

What a good decision it turned out to be. That treatment saved not only my teeth, but also my time inside.

When asked at my first check-up in Silivri whether I was under any medical treatment, I'd replied, 'My teeth.'

Ordinary dental treatments are carried out in the prison; but specialist intervention like orthodontics, for instance, requires the 'patient' to be sent to the Istanbul University School of Dentistry at Çapa.

My pass was written, my orthodontist was informed and the patient was despatched to the hospital in a prisoner transport van one Wednesday morning. One first lieutenant, one driver, one warder, three gendarmes and I set off for Çapa, where a further three gendarme intelligence officers joined up, making up a big team of ten.

As the prisoner transport van proceeded down the emergency lane, lights flashing, siren cleaving through the traffic, the patient inside was happily murmuring a song about a rare type of crane, amused at the pun on braces suggested by its crest.

It was impossible to mingle with the public on the way to and back from court hearings; but hospital visits entailed a few steps between the parked vehicle and the building, passing between patients, possibility of contact and conversation with doctors and the opportunity to breathe in civilian life, albeit in part.

When we had parked outside the hospital and the gendarmes leapt down, they hesitated about grabbing my arms; the commander saw no need and they fell back.

Before I was arrested, my friends and family had been advising me to engage protection; and here I was, with just about the best protection team you could wish for, now that I was a prisoner.

We made our way to the hospital through a group enjoying

their cigarettes. It was impossible for me to stay unnoticed with my gendarme contingent. People started waving and cheering, and trying to get closer to talk. Some were moved to tears as others cursed those who'd locked me up.

I was mixing with people for the first time in a month, albeit behind a wall of protection. I felt that love soak through to my bones; I stored and recorded it.

Some called out, 'So sorry' or 'God save you'; others approached, 'We're with you,' and wanted to pose for photos. The gendarmes politely asked them to get back.

The first lieutenant whispered, 'Please don't misunderstand; it's just to protect you.'

'Except, it's those above I need protection from,' I replied.

I was handed over to a beautiful doctor, who looked quite busy. The first thing she did was to look at my wrists to see if I was handcuffed, before asking what I needed.

'I've got braces,' I said. 'I would like to continue the treatment.'

She asked me to wait for a while in an indifferent attitude. I asked if it were possibly to notify my own orthodontist at the Okan University School of Dentistry.

'We'll see,' she replied.

I was a little upset.

She must have noticed: 'Come along, let's get your appointments sorted,' she said, leading me to reception. On the steps, she leant towards my ear to whisper, 'Don't worry, Can Bey, you're in safe hands.'

She was my tooth fairy. She'd come to rescue me. All I could do was stammer a delighted thanks.

My appointments were arranged, doctors flocked over, I shook hands reaching out fondly, breathed in the air of shared emotions and chatted briefly.

I had to admit to a first: hurrying to a dental appointment with such enthusiasm. Suddenly my teeth had become my favourite organs. I had found a way of getting out of Silivri 'by the skin of my teeth', as if I'd dug a legal tunnel out.

Çapa became my lifeline, my anchor, as its name suggested.

Now every Wednesday I'd get ready as if going to a festival, pass amongst smiling faces and, thanks to the warm attention of the dentistry staff, enjoy civilian life, even if only for a couple of hours.

Kindness...

That's what keeps you going when you're in prison.

It might not be able to oppose injustice openly, but it wholeheartedly tries to support the wronged and offer a modicum of happiness.

This shared heart, this mobilisation of love injects the jailbird with enough encouragement to last a lifetime, regardless of the attempts to sentence him to lovelessness.

Grabbing the ivy held down into your heart for solidarity, you climb over walls. And realise that it's not money or things you need to accumulate throughout your life, that there is no greater treasure than friends.

I have seen such extraordinary examples of this fact.

My newspaper kept us in the news by reporting daily. One hundred and fifty lawyers and MPs hurried over in the first thirty days, in the worst of the winter, just so we wouldn't feel alone.

A close friend completed his – previously interrupted – legal internship just so he could visit me as a lawyer. One of our solicitors secretly placed in my hand a bar of chocolate he'd snuck in; I took a lusty joy in melting it against the roof of my mouth.

I was to learn later that a very close friend had tried to get the supplier to include Nutella on the list when he found out that the canteen didn't stock it as he knew, 'Can Abi likes it!'

Saying, 'I'm too old to come to the Vigil of Hope; instead, I'm sending you this painting,' a famous artist made history with his 'Resistance' as the first work of art to hold vigil at the prison gate. It now hangs behind my head in my office.

My favourite musicians sang resistance songs at the gate.

A singer I adore sent me a song he'd written to commemorate my imprisonment.

Young directors dedicated their awards as they stood on the

stage in the ceremonies, knowing full well they might never receive another.

A group of stage actors came right to the Silivri wall and yelled with all their might, 'You're not alone!'

A group of poets took poetry to the streets as they recited verses in stentorian tones outside the gate of the clink.

Some sent us greetings on every morning show; others put a counter in their columns to mark the days, republished my old columns on their own pages and dedicated meaningful songs on YouTube.

Friends outside started petitions to make our voices heard around the world.

Mothers sent in jumpers, socks and caps they'd knitted and MPs brought in long underwear, while doctors sent good nutrition guides and yogis posted practice books so I could stay fit. Journalists marched for thirty steps on the thirtieth day of our incarceration to keep the number of days in public memory and the *BirGün* published a supplement in solidarity.

City councils and societies handed out their prizes at the Silivri gate.

Eleven Consul-Generals whom I'd never even seen visited the *Cumhuriyet* and signed a declaration.

Someone who wanted to send a pair of budgies to keep me company changed her mind so I wouldn't be imprisoning the birds.

Someone else tried to bring Cinnamon to the hospital gate, knowing I must miss him.

Nebil Özgentürk mobilised the crew to complete the interrupted Cuba documentary. I wrote the script and sent it out; Ege did the voice-over instead of me. When a summary was broadcast in the news, it strengthened me all the more.

A friend who has a prosthetic leg asked during our open visit what I missed most.

'A glass of rakı wouldn't go amiss!' I said.

'I'll try to sneak one in inside my leg next time,' he grinned.

Let me go back to the beginning.

On our way back from the orthodontist that day, the young gendarme in the protection squad was just about to search me and hand me over to the warders when he leant down to my ear and said, 'Abi, let me give you a hug as I search you, but don't hug me back, OK?'

But it was a reflex; I couldn't resist it.

I hugged him back.

We were in such a place that…

One side was shedding leaves, the other was a spring garden…[38]

30

COLOUR

SILIVRI HAS quite a long list of bans.

Rugs are forbidden, for instance. Curtains, duvets and heaters are forbidden.

Wearing a tracksuit to a legal visit is forbidden, as are hanging anything on the walls, placing a lamp on the table, or using a typewriter.

Soil or potted plants in the cell are forbidden.

Reading a book during transport or chatting with the other prisoners is forbidden.

One of the things I missed most was colour.

Silivri is devoid of colour too, just as it is of rakı, jewellery, scents or textures; it almost qualifies as a specially decoloured zone.

Or, more accurately, only dull colours are allowed: military khaki, warder navy and concrete grey are allowed.

Interior walls are dirty yellow, iron doors are brown, floor tiles are beige and the kitchen worktop is metal.

The plastic table and chair are pale white. As is the light of the fluorescent strip.

There is no other colour.

The sea is distant, the sky is imprisoned.

If you wanted to draw a daisy to send someone, you couldn't find any yellow; coloured pens are not allowed. You can't cover the dirty yellow as hanging posters on the walls is forbidden.

More interestingly, popular colours here are denied to us: you can't bring in a khaki jumper or a navy blue jacket for example, to stop us escaping by pretending to be penitentiary officers or soldiers.

In other words, even colours are imprisoned here along with us.

But where people live, there will be colour.

Thankfully, friends and family posted colourful envelopes and sheets and pads of paper the moment they heard. My *Cumhuriyet* colleague Selin Ongun sent in a couple of fleeces, one turquoise and the other orange. I grabbed the turquoise. A reader sent in his nature photographs; I festooned the grey worktop with grass, flowers and trees. I created a pastoral style in the cell.

The more you are restricted, the more determined you become to break free. This determination can only be assuaged by full freedom; it brooks no wall.

One of the first things I'd planned to do the moment I was banged up was to publish a *Green Silivri* magazine, given the variety of the ideological range inside and the even wider scope it had the potential to attain with future additions to the team. Later, a solicitor told me about the Wild Waves Outside initiative.

Then came their letters.

Wild Waves started out as a bridge of books between those inside and outside. Books were sent to prisoners in solitary in response to the practice that began in the 2000s.

This entirely voluntary effort delivered tens of thousands of books to prisons. In time, Wild Waves grew to hold exhibitions of prisoner's paintings, whose sales funded the publication of stories written by inmates in cells. And finally, they enabled correspondence between twenty or so famous writers with imprisoned fellow litterateurs.

The greatest obstacle of course is censorship in prison. Silivri boasts a fine library, but most of the shelves are empty. Erdem and I donated the majority of the books we'd received to fill them, but we heard that they'd been taken into storage for inspection.

It might take months for a committee to read them and pass judgment on their suitability to rehabilitate prisoners. The funny thing was, four of my books were actually held in the Silivri library! Spotting them in the list gave me a bittersweet pride of being both sickness and cure: I could read my own writing to be 'rehabilitated' in the prison in which I was held for what I had written.

I read the convicted Wild Waves writers instead. Their tips proved very useful.

I learnt how to make soil out of brewed tea leaves and plant flowers from seeds snuck in, how to use a long piece of string to retrieve a kite snagged on the wire and how to produce colour by breaching the coloured pen ban.

That last one proved especially helpful.

A lawyer explained how coloured newsprint was stuck on steamed glass, and the dripping ink then scraped off using a razor blade. It was an ingenious method. Needless to say, I tried it straight away.

I'd never put colour supplements to such good use, or the tabloid press in general. I pressed the magazine supplements against the windowpanes.

First, I distilled yellow for the daisy from the coat of the 'famous society bride'. Then dipped into the red jacket of an Istanbul jet-set crown prince to paint a rose.

I felt like a Robin Hood stealing colours from the rich for his humble abode. Like scraping a black canvas to paint a colourful land. Not satisfied, I attacked the fruit next.

Dipping my toothbrush into orange scraped from orange peel, burgundy from radishes and green from apples, I painted 'June protest', a staircase in the ruled notebook.

That's how I overcame the colour ban. They want to cage us, the public, the nation and the world, into a single colour.

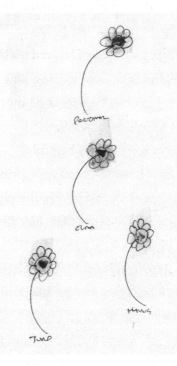

'June protest'

Only one chief should be allowed to speak, and to universal accolades at that, so there isn't a single objection.

They are scared of every colour that defies this uniformity.

They want everyone to drop all colours and kneel, waving a white flag.

They are scared that their khaki-and-navy rule might be erased by a rainbow.

What they don't know is that this nation is capable of distilling inks from fruit peel when they set their mind to it; capable of wielding a toothbrush as a paintbrush and making June into the month of rebellion. We might like a single measure of rakı, but we don't like to be forced into a single lane…

We subscribe to the idea of a 'colourful' world; we do not submit to the grey of lead, walls or smoke.

As you would have seen in the case of the academics who defied Erdoğan: the more you oppress, the more we will rise. Draw red crosses on their doors and they will draw up defiant manifestos.

The cameraman in the white-flag-bearing delegation will film his own blood when he is shot and broadcast it to the world.

Wherever you go, whomever you talk to, you will be asked about us.

Say, 'Saying dictator is forbidden!' all you want; opponents of your oppression will deliberately call you a dictator.

Your Unauthorised Palace is protected by salaried policemen, whereas our concentration camp gate is stage to a vigil by our volunteers, our comrades.

Make them pay the heaviest price if you like; they will still write what they know to be right.

You cannot defeat us.

31

PARCEL

HAPPINESS IN Silivri knocks on your door at certain times:

'Got a visitor!'

'Got a letter!'

'Got a parcel!'

Visit and post days are fixed, but you never know when your parcel will be delivered. There are times when nothing is handed out for a fortnight. I asked why.

'It depends on the dog,' I was told.

It appears a sniffer dog checks the parcels arriving at the prison. Occasionally, his workload is too much to keep up with, so our parcels have to wait their turn.

This snippet made me murmur, 'Vahim! I bet it's him.'

The prosecutors and gendarmes who intercepted the MİT lorries weren't the only ones to have been demoted and worse.

The sniffer dog that had participated in the operation and discovered munitions (and not humanitarian aid) had also been exiled.

His name was Vahim. Rhymes with, and means, grim.

'I bet he's in a grim state, too,' I thought.

It occurred to me that Vahim Grim could have been banished to the Silivri Parcel Sniffing Section.

Chances are, he too was a lifer…

Anyway, this is what happens once your parcel has passed the sniffing test: the hatch in your door opens. A mouth shouts in:

'Can Dündar! Got a parcel.'

This is almost as good as hearing Father Christmas is here to visit me.

You exit your cell and are searched as usual; you are then escorted by two warders to a parcel delivery desk overseen by a ten-man committee comprising a penitentiary protection officer and several gendarmes. And gift parcels on the desk…

Your parcels are opened before this committee, as if viewing the gifts at a wedding.

'Ten books from the publisher…'

'Five parcels from the newspaper…'

'Underwear sent by X…'

The main difference between this ceremony and the thrill of opening presents under the tree is that here, someone else opens yours... All you derive is a vicarious pleasure, and from a distance at that.

One official notes down the cargo number of the parcel, the name of the sender and the date of despatch, and gets you to sign this record. Then another opens the parcel.

They're mostly books. Occasionally a notebook might emerge, or a pen, notepad, jumper, cardigan, scarf, pyjamas or underwear.

A ceremony you watch now with longing, now with a smile. Some parcels bear best friends' names as senders, others come from perfect strangers. Some parcels reveal the cheekiest, naughtiest presents, whereas others offer essentials...

Don't think all you do next is tuck your presents under your arm and return to your cell, like coming back from festive season shopping.

They're mostly seized.

The books are checked for hidden messages (this involves turning them upside down and shaking) in front of you and then sent to Inspection before being handed over.

Since you are forbidden to receive anything that might be sold in the canteen, nothing of the pen or spiral-bound notebook type is handed over, although the occasional notepad might be allowed.

You have a quota on jumpers, cardigans and shirts. You're only allowed three jumpers; when a fourth arrives, you can only take possession of it on condition that you return one of the other three. You can't be allowed to build up a wardrobe or anything inside. That's not to say there isn't a burgeoning wardrobe in your name, albeit independently of you. Take me, for example: at my release, my store revealed jumpers, cardigans, hot water bottles, plasters, worry beads and stress balls.

Duvet sets are forbidden too. Apparently they can be dipped in drugs, dried without rinsing and sent in. The inmates would then soak them and get high. So I'm told by the parcel team.

A blue envelope bearing a white sheet arrived in the post last month. Four lines of handwriting on the sheet:

'A memento from my father's drawer, hoping it might warm you up. Nükhet'

Sadly the envelope held nothing more.

A sheet taped to the envelope stated: '1 "Handkerchief" was enclosed in the envelope. The handkerchief was handed over to Safekeeping.'

Of course I got it. This was Abdi İpekçi's handkerchief.

His daughter Nükhet must have sent it in when she came to Silivri on vigil. Whatever peril the inspection committee must have detected in the handkerchief, they had taken the decision to consign this priceless gift to Safekeeping. I was quite upset.

On 1 February, that is, the anniversary of his assassination, I paid tribute to the editor-in-chief of the *Milliyet*. He was younger than I am now, the editor-in-chief of the *Cumhuriyet*.

That's how I had taken over the accursed flag.

It took a while, but the charge that had left his desk drawer and come to me thirty-seven years later was eventually handed over by Safekeeping.

While we were incarcerated, the tiny vigil tent outside the Silivri gate played host to the loved ones of our masters who had fallen victim to the epidemic of hatred that was handed down from generation to generation:

Nükhet İpekçi.

Güldal Mumcu.[39]

Dolunay Kışlalı.

Zeynep Altıok.

As they kept watch, we endeavoured to carry the flag they had entrusted to us, and carry it in a manner that did them justice.

Their principles were etched in our minds, and their charges were in our hearts.

32

ERDEM

MURAT SABUNCU, our news coordinator who ran the *Cumhuriyet* for a while, had offered some advice when I was appointed editor-in-chief, which included the following: 'The editor-in-chief and the Ankara bureau chief must talk several times a day…'

One day when he came to visit, he reminded me of his advice with a belly laugh: 'That's what I said, but I didn't mean stay together 24/7!'

Erdem and I shared twenty-four hours a day for fifty-two days.

I had never lived cheek-by-jowl with anyone for such a long time under such intense conditions. I don't think he had either.

At first, we were placed in adjacent cells and prevented from contact. It was three weeks later when we were first allowed to meet, and that was during sports.

We hugged inside a box of 10 sq. m topped with a ceiling of sky. We must have completed close to 200 laps around that artificial turf pitch in that hour and a half. We spoke non-stop of imprisonment, solitary confinement, court, families, justice and the newspaper, and did so with the insatiable appetite of those thirsting for conversation.

We were now allowed sports twice a week under the CCTV cameras: an open-air artificial turf pitch on Mondays and indoor volleyball court on Wednesdays.

Other inmates held on charges of 'membership of an organisation' could hold five-a-side matches; we, on the other hand, charged not with membership but with 'aiding and abetting', couldn't form teams. All we could do was kick and catch a ball between the two of us. So the price of espionage was being alone on the pitch. It meant individual sports.

But we had other advantages. We went all out. Or, rather, Erdem still played like the classy athlete he was, but I took all my rage out on the ball. You'd have thought I was kicking someone's head in.

The harder I kicked, the higher the ball rose; I ended up kicking the ball up to the roof or into the wires. Then these two newspaper editors had to wait for the warders to bring back our ball, downhearted like kids whose kite was snagged on the cables. Two of our footballs on the roof of Silivri are still waiting to be fetched back.

After we'd completed a month in solitary, experienced lawyers cautioned us.

'The first month goes by in a flash; it's only after six weeks that solitary really gets you.'

They were right: the first month – effectively an internship – simply flew by. I might have awoken every once in a while wondering what I was doing here or if I was really in prison, but on the whole solitude served me well. My work was quite productive, and I got used to the 'bachelor lifestyle'.

On 4 January, with an, 'I've got good news for you,' the Warden ended our solitary confinement. Half an hour later, my neighbour Erdem moved in with all his belongings.

To be honest we weren't all that close. Didn't really know what the other was like. Like most, I'd only really seen him on the screen.

Two journalists who might have only sat together at a dinner would now live in the same room for goodness knew how many days, weeks, months or years.

He was a revolutionary, the son of a TÖB-DER[40] man. His father had been imprisoned but he had not.

We had thronged the same plazas wearing the same parkas in the years before Ankara was changed beyond recognition by Gökçek. As some founded religious brotherhoods, our

Together and side by side for twenty-four
hours a day for fifty-two days…

brothers and we set up barricades. And now we were imprisoned by the founders of brotherhoods.

A few days later, I was convinced this was the best person to share my troubles. Erdem was a true comrade, as virtuous as his name suggested.

Imagine living with someone – even if that is your favourite person in the world – in a small room throughout the day, eating all three meals together, working on two plastic tables placed side by side, using the same bathroom next to the tables, sharing one single TV set, fridge, and your solitary isolation, sleeping and awaking in beds next to each other; that's when the real importance of this harmony comes into play.

I now had direct and immediate access to his political

commentary that everyone else had been watching on TV debates. And I was his sole viewer here.

He was a true Ankara journalist who had been breathing politics for years. He seemed to subsist on books, newspapers and cigarettes.

As soon as he had arrived, we turned the nook under the stairs into a library. I wouldn't allow the pool media into our 'home', but, thanks to Erdem, we started getting them too.

He would start the day reading the 'crony media' with a curiosity I sometimes found verging on the masochistic before giving me a sardonic summary of the catastrophes awaiting us.

We held political and legal debates, listened to and sang songs when we got tired, and watched football on weekends.

I must confess to having decided at the time of my arrest to avoid the mind-numbing TV debates and the stifling pages of the newspapers. I would use this incarceration as an opportunity for an intellectual detox.

The avid reader had overtaken the journalist.

True, I still waited for the papers eagerly, but it felt better to bury myself in books after a cursory glance at the news. Books bathed my soul. Chance would have been a fine thing anywhere else.

After reading and writing all day, I would cast a look at the news in the evening, click through a couple of soaps so as to keep up with popular culture and watch a film instead of a debate.

Erdem's mind, on the other hand, was justifiably on politics. We had a single TV set and a single remote controller. At first we checked to see what was being discussed in his absence. His absence was palpable.

Later I began to tempt him. The moment any debate foundered, I zapped us towards a film.

I summarised a few for his benefit, and made him watch a few. Even introduced him to Zuhal Topal's matchmaking show as we waited for Fox News.

True, it was not politics *per se*, but what it did portray was the society in its most naked state. The brief life stories – no more than five or ten minutes – of those seeking a life partner ran like a series of short tragedies, laying bare the patchwork of a society flailing between deeply entrenched conservatism and modernism that has caught them unawares, a society whose suppressed sexuality spilt over its eternal fanaticism.

As we waited for the news, Erdem was forced to listen to the matchmaking show's permanent studio guests: the scrapping of Hanife and Umur, and Şendoğan Abi's attempts at arbitration, instead of his usual fare of government-opposition arguments.

He would raise his head from his book in an orderly fashion I was so familiar with from my days in the capital, glance quizzically at this world that had never piqued his interest before, and the more he was surprised, the faster he clicked his worry beads.

After this sociology bulletin that offered deep family secrets came the unpalatable news of the nation's politics.

Hell lay beyond the wall.

One thousand people had been killed since the June elections, and the country was now a terrifying fire scene.

The screens screamed. The public soaked up pain like a sponge, soaked it up but never spat it out.

Our souls were seared with the pain of the outside as we forgot we were inside. It was almost embarrassing to complain of our own condition.

But we had been shoved into a well of injustice.

We had appealed to the majority of the ten criminal courts, and each time we had crashed into high walls of palace stone.

Our petitions weren't even read.

It was like the order was already in their hands in written form: 'The appeal for release is rejected...'

We didn't even feel the need to go to the courthouse. Silivri's audio visual IT system offered its inmates the opportunity for remote control rejection on the spot without trundling over to the courthouse.

You went upstairs, faced a screen in a small studio, were connected to the courthouse and saw the judge before you, answered the perfunctory questions he posed, obtained an order for the continuation of your detention and returned to your cell.

No courtroom, no prosecutor, no defence, no public.

The order followed in writing: 'Rejected!'

The criminal courts founded to facilitate the government's total domination of the justice system were an institution of injustice – presided over by stereotypical judges – that would inspire anyone to write a novel entitled *Crime and Justice*.

Such a flawless Captivetown had been created in Silivri that you could languish in its prison, be tried in its courts, be fed from its kitchens, do your sports on its pitches, be treated in its hospital, pray in its mosque, raise your children in its school and be buried in a cemetery nearby when you died.

The scissors between justice and law were open all the way, cutting through our skin.

We had no idea how much longer we would stay imprisoned.

No matter how patient, phlegmatic and solid he was, Erdem had a tougher time of it than I, since his sons were quite young.

He might be doing his best to keep the relationship warm through notebooks filled with memoirs, fairy tales and stories; but he wasn't unaware of the abyss in their little hearts.

It wasn't exactly a festival for us either...

So we'd become Mustafa Keser's[41] soldiers to cheer ourselves up; washing up joyfully, spearing the black dust bunnies that spontaneously emerged every other day with our Viledas, tipping the oily dishes down the loo and spooning the canteen-bought meat sauté on bulgur seasoned with spices into some semblance of flavour.

We might repeat the need to be prepared for a long stay, although in our heart of hearts we probably didn't really feel it. We simply avoided voicing it out loud.

I sought solace in sleep when we got too melancholy, and he in cigarettes.

Mindful of his non-smoker cell-mate, he went out into the yard in daytime and stood at the window at nights so he could puff his worries out through the bars without bothering me.

It was on 27 January, three weeks after Erdem's move, that our indictment was read.

I was out on an orthodontic appointment that day. That's where I heard the news.

It was delivered as mournfully as news of a death: 'They're seeking two life sentences for you, one aggravated. Plus a thirty-year sentence.'

This was equivalent to the old death sentence.

This was the sentence sought for Öcalan.

Ignoring guidance, the prosecutor had pushed as hard as he could. My yell of joy astonished those around me at the hospital.

What mattered was not the sentence sought, but that the indictment was ready. Some people had been kept waiting for years ostensibly for the 'preparation of the indictment'.

The demand for a sentence long enough that I might even be reincarnated was to curry favour with the palace:

'I'd have taken him seriously if the prosecutor had sought a couple of years, but this multiple life sentence lunacy only shows we'll be out soon,' I said.

In a land where suicide bombers get thirty years maximum, and murder suspects are tried without detention, the gravity of the sentence hanging over us was proof of the greatness of their fear.

A glance at the 473-page indictment only reinforced this appraisal.

The text included fifty-two of my articles. Prosecutor Fidan had published a collection of my articles without my approval. What he had failed to explain was what they served to demonstrate. Confusing me with his own position, he had claimed they had been written 'under instruction'; he had found no proof of our 'guilt' other than these articles. What he had offered, however, was the best proof that we were being tried on charges of journalism.

The news reports on the MİT lorries had not been deemed sufficient; my articles on the 17–25 December corruption scandal were included, as they also needed avenging.

28 January 2016

A universally known topic somehow sent me to the gallows when I covered it in the *Cumhuriyet*; far from being an indictment for my paper or me, this was a commendation.

But legally it was a total fiasco.

The terror section of the indictment was an unauthorised excerpt cut and pasted from a previously published academic paper, dating the origins of our crime to 66AD.

This dull text that started with the Zealots only managed to hold my interest for a few pages. I put it aside.

Erdem read it carefully, the diligent journalist that he is, and summarised it for me. It was empty.

Blank. Void.

We were paying for exposing an 'open secret'.

In the old penal system of wards, we two 'gallows birds' would have risen to rule the ward. But, in isolation, we were two lifers stuffed into an area of 10 sq. m.

Akın came to visit in the evening.

Erdem and I might now share quarters, but we still couldn't see our solicitor together. Here was yet another anomaly. Legal counsel would have to explain everything to us individually.

Despite maintaining his constant cautiousness and avoiding any false hope, Akın was quite optimistic:

'Today, our case file is largely out of the palace control. We are now in the "normal" legal process. There now are two possibilities: either the Constitutional Court will deliberate on the indictment and end your detention, or the fourteenth criminal court will accept the indictment within a fortnight, announce a hearing date and release you at the first hearing. You will be out in the spring.'

On 5 February, we heard on TV that the indictment was accepted and that the hearing was set for 25 March.

We started marking dawns like national servicemen counting down to their discharge: we had been in for seventy days, and had fifty more to go.

The uncertainty was coming to an end and the process

moved more swiftly than we had guessed. Balbay and journalists Tuncay Özkan, Nedim and Ahmet had waited for months and years to reach the point we'd got to in a matter of weeks.

I was happy that we had an idea of what the future held at the very least. I also expected a move from the Constitutional Court before the hearing date.

Erdem was cautious; he wasn't that happy with the idea of having to spend another fifty days inside. Since he followed the pro-government media closely, he was aware of the disquiet at this swift progress, and therefore worried about the prospect of some plot to prevent our release.

Of course it was possible.

They must have learnt from their erstwhile partners the finer details of engineering plots. No stone would be left unturned to bring pressure to bear on the Constitutional Court and the fourteenth criminal court to find some dirty way of keeping us inside.

This could drag on or end quite quickly depending on the power play in politics.

We were ready, but the newspaper was exhausted.

Editorial had been working flat out in an unforgettable display of loyalty; no one went on leave for the past two months as staff did their best to support both the *Cumhuriyet* and us.

With two key managers inside, they were busy publishing a newspaper without fail, shouldering the legal struggle, hosting visiting delegations, coping with problems piling up and implementing radical decisions that had lingered for far too long.

I'd told Erdem at one of our earliest sports sessions that I had to resign. I couldn't leave the newspaper without an editor during an indeterminate period of detention. I could at least resign as editor-in-chief and thereby enable new management. This would alleviate my own mental burden as well as clear the way for the paper.

I fully subscribed to the view that the greed for power is the greatest slavery of all and that the freedom to relinquish is a far greater freedom. At least this way I would be liberated from one count of captivity. Erdem did see my point of view, albeit reluctantly.

On the day that the indictment was accepted, I wrote to the foundation governing the newspaper, and then I penned a column for the paper for publication on 8 February.

That was the first anniversary of my tenure as editor-in-chief of the *Cumhuriyet*. It made sense to resign on that date.

I thanked my readers and colleagues, and ended the column with my reasons for wanting to be excused from the post of editor-in-chief.

On the next day, I opened the paper to see that the gratitude section was published but the resignation had been axed.

The newspaper I managed had censored me.

Bugün 8 Şubat Pazartesi...

GEÇEN sene tam bugün Cumhuriyet'in Genel Yayın
Yönetmeni olarak göreve başlamıştım. 2.5 aydır
Erdem Gül ve ben, Silivri'de Cumhuriyetimizin
okuru durumundayız. Ama yol arkadaşlarımız,
gayretle ve cesaretle gemimizi açık
denizlere sürdüler, sürüyorlar.

Akın came over again. He explained why they didn't publish the last section with a smile: 'You think we'll let you go that easily? Wait for the trial to start; let's see how things progress, and then we can assess the situation.'

He was convinced it wouldn't drag on. And, indeed, I read the good news in the *Cumhuriyet* dated Saturday 13 February: the Constitutional Court would review our petition on 17 February.

I was flying.

I started packing without noticing.

See? We were leaving...

Erdem was still asleep. I wondered if I should awaken him with the good news. Then I worried about some cautious remark of his that might take the wind out of my sails. Which is precisely what happened.

I shouted, 'Great news; we're going out!' when he awoke, but he wasn't as thrilled as I was. He read the report sceptically.

'If the Constitutional Court were to debate and reject

our petition before the criminal court, we'd have no hope of release at the trial either.'

I was deflated. From that moment forth, we turned into two lifers in the cell, one an optimist, and the other a pessimist.

My calendar was set to 17 February; I was counting down the hours. Erdem was counting to 25 March, as if the Constitutional Court weren't there. His dawn was forty, mine was four.

I thought the Constitutional Court would take the historic decision and release not only us but other journalists as well, thereby alleviating Turkey as it faced increased pressure from the West.

Suspecting an arm-wrestling match behind an Erdoğan–Gül tussle, Erdem was trying to avoid any untimely optimism. Cem Küçük was already blackmailing the Constitutional Court members. You could count on nothing in a country where the law was under such oppression.

Of course his view was quite realistic. The higher your hopes, the harder you would fall.

But I was one of those who'd rather soar as high as possible if only to crash head first instead of cautiously floating parallel to the ground.

What was the point of flying if you didn't risk a crash?

What mattered was refusing to surrender to Big Brother.

George Orwell relates how an oppressive regime convinces people to believe that two and two made five.

At the end of the book, Winston Smith's finger writes 2+2=5 in the dust on the desk. This is the scene where he surrenders. We wouldn't make the same mistake. We wouldn't surrender to a lie.

Anyone who went inside after us would only find resolve and the inscription 'Freedom' there.

33

LOVE

JULIUS FUČIK was arrested by the Nazis on a warm spring evening.

He was the editor-in-chief of the Czechoslovakian Communist Party newspaper, and one of the leaders of the resistance.

He was subjected to terrible torture in prison. He didn't talk.

Six weeks later, the Nazis tried a different method to break his resistance. At 3 a.m., they brought his wife Augusta into his cell. She thought he had already been killed.

As she stood, astonished, the Nazi commissioner asked, 'Do you recognise him?'

The man she faced was all but unrecognisable; not for her, of course. Fučik attempted to swallow the blood around his mouth so she wouldn't notice. In vain, however: the blood was on every part of his face, dripping down to his fingertips.

Augusta's gaze didn't betray her terror as she replied, 'No, I don't.' Unconvinced, the commissioner pushed her closer to the bloodied face.

'Convince him,' he said. 'Convince him to pull himself together. He's not thinking of himself, but he might at least think of you. You have an hour. Think hard. If you continue to stick to your guns, you'll both face the firing squad tonight...'

Augusta's eyes stroked her husband as she spoke: 'You can't threaten me. My last and greatest wish is this: if you're going to shoot him, you'll have to shoot me too.'

Fučik tried to smile, an abortive farewell smile that drowned in his bleeding mouth. Augusta was taken away.

That was the last time the lovers saw each other.

Augusta was sent to a concentration camp in Poland about a year later. Sentenced to death in August 1943, Fučik was hanged in Berlin on 8 September.

Augusta was amongst the surviving inmates the fascists hadn't yet got round to torturing to death in the spring of 1945, when Hitler was routed. She was little more than a bag of bones at her liberation.

She returned to Czechoslovakia straight away to look for her husband, and heard that he'd been executed. But there was one more thing: Fučik had written notes on cigarette papers and pages from a notebook smuggled in by a Czech warder when he was imprisoned in Prague. He had numbered each one and had them smuggled to friends outside. No one person had more than one page.

Augusta found the warder first, and took the notes he still had. Then she set off on the trail of the rest. She gathered the numbered sheets concealed by loyal friends. These lines were written under the shadow of the gallows. She devoured those small sheets that wracked her heart.

Her husband had written after that meeting in his cell:

> That's my Gusta; a magnificent love and a terrific force…
>
> They might take our lives, can't they, Gusta? But they can't take our love or our pride.
>
> They didn't even allow us to say goodbye, hug or even just hold hands. You and I both know that we will never see each other again in all likelihood. All the same, I can hear you calling out:
>
> Goodbye my love!
>
> Farewell for now…

Fučik's farewell to his wife still had a hopeful postscript:

> Imagine how we would live if we could be reunited once all this was behind us! To meet again in freedom, in a life glorified by creative freedom… When we finally attain all that we'd longed for, all that we'd patiently

worked towards, and all that we're now going to death for…

Even if we're not alive [on that day] we will still be living
in an infinitesimal particle of human happiness. Difficult as
parting is, this [possibility] is still a soothing one.[42]

Augusta published these notes in her free country. They were
translated and published in many others. In Turkish, they
were published by Yordam Kitap in Celal Üster's wonderful
translation. And reached me in my cell.

I paid homage to Valentine's Day with Fučik and his Gusta's
eternal love as befitting a prisoner behind bars.

It behoves us to remember human happiness has been seasoned with their own blood and love.

Love is resistance.

We'll never give up.

34

THEATRE

WHEN IT comes to literacy, Silivri Prison might well rank amongst the top in Turkey.

The majority of us in high-security section are all educated, at the very least. The occupancy rates are equally high. This could easily be an ideal venue for a theatre troupe.

On 16 February, Silivri Prison played host to the first stage play in its history. Happily, we were the first audience in that performance. The residents of A1 Street…

The play was *The Last Birds*, an adaptation of a Sait Faik short story. A joint State Theatre/General Directorate of Penitentiaries project aimed to bring the theatre to 180,000 inmates and 200,000 staff in 223 prisons.

The posters had been hung in the corridors days before the performance, and the warders had come to the door to ask if we would attend.

Erdem wasn't too keen. But I leapt at the chance straight away.

I made good use of every opportunity to leave the cell; and watching a play would be a blessing in its own right. What I was really curious about, though, was how the inmates in solitary would be able to watch a play. We were totally forbidden to get together, you see.

When the day came, we were taken to the hall where we met visiting MPs. The plastic chairs were arranged in several rows and the freed space facing them had become a make-shift stage.

The décor consisted of iron bars fixed to the floor by means of a bench.

A scene from *The Last Birds*; Turgay Tanülkü second from left

Again?

Yes.

The first play staged in prison was set in a dungeon. A prisoner was in the lead part.

It seemed that the repertoire was based on the notion that learning about another world would have been detrimental. The idea that watching those in far worse situations than us would have made us count our blessings.

Soon the audience trickled in. The judge in A1 was here, but the prosecutor in A2 and the governor in A4 were not. My insistence had paid off; Erdem was here, which enabled him to meet the police officers in A6 and the colonel in A8.

That was the sum total of the audience.

We had been neighbours for weeks, and might even have locked eyes through the little windows as we passed down the corridors; but this was the first time we met in person and shook hands.

The troupe was practically more crowded than the audience: three actors, one singer, the lighting man and the soundman.

Once the lights went down and a prison play started in a prison, we were immersed in the joy of breathing in life and art at the same time.

Actor Turgay Tanülkü, who also directed the play, had been involved with the theatre for prisoners since 1981. It was his responsibility to train prisoner actors and recruit them into his troupe.

This particular play had been staged for a total of 65,000 detainees and convicts. *The Last Birds* was the final tour of his career on the stage.

So sincere was his acting, so heartfelt the tears dripping from the eyes of the convict in the cell on stage that they drowned us, the audience, in tears of our own. As the singer sang, 'Precious crane, send my greetings to the home of my sweetheart / tell her not to cry, I might get there yet,' longing flooded the hall.

An intense sediment of melancholy weighed us down as we left. It was heartbreaking to see our own lives repeated on stage. Still, it was better than the theatre at our criminal court hearings.

As Tanülkü reminded us in our brief chat after the play, every visit was a stage play in actual fact… Everyone knew that a single teardrop outside would cause a flood of tears inside, and vice versa.

That is why both the visitor and the detainee starts preparing early in the morning, rehearsing how not to release any tears that might be welling up, brushing hair, trimming nails and choosing a smart outfit. Memorising what needs to be said so nothing is forgotten, and opening sentences with a stock phrase, 'You're looking well.'

The obligation to cheer each other up forces sorrow into a nook of the face, hidden behind smiles.

So a double play was acted out on both sides of the glass.

An hour-long play – exciting, tragic and enervating...

Once it was over, the exhausted parties (actor and audience at the same time) left, one for home, the other for the cell; the make-up came off and the actors assumed their natural states.

Once this stageless play was over, hopeful lines lingered on the glass, on the telephone cables and the walls of the visit room.

The play was over once the telephone line went dead.

Curtain!

35

THE SUN

WE'D BEEN inside for less than ten days.

As I was flicking through the papers, my eye caught Hakan Kırkoğlu's astrology section in the *Milliyet* supplement.

He'd checked my stars, and began with, 'He's got a hard task.' He might have meant it well, but his news was less good: Saturn – that had been moving towards Capricorn since the end of 2014 – was crossing my Gemini, and things were about to get harder for me. It would take until late 2017 for Saturn to leave Capricorn.

In short, things didn't look that bright for me until September 2017.

Although I wasn't particularly thrilled at the prospect of distant stars pulling the rug under my feet as I counted the days inside, I wasn't discouraged either. Quite the opposite,

I went into a more aggressive mode: 'I'll give those planets what for!'

It is true that what doesn't kill you makes you stronger.

There was no horizon in the cell. Just like our steps, our gaze slammed against a wall no matter which way we turned. Which is why every evening, before the warders came to remove from our sight the fading sky, its blue face paling, we gazed at that oblong sky long and hard, gazed to our fill.

The map I saw in that oblong sky told me something completely different: 'If you believe you only have one life, try to live it properly. If you have had a good life, one is enough. The rest is up to Saturn.'

All the same, the oracle giving me news from the stars managed to sneak into a corner of the mind and becalm the enthusiasm that constantly packed a case, 'Stay where you are; you're here for quite a while yet.'

It wasn't loneliness. I'd tried it myself; if there was a crowd outside, loneliness didn't hurt.

What hurt was hope.

When hope arrived, it settled, leaving no room for despair. That was the most dangerous poison inside: hope.

A couple of doses and your feet left the ground. The pigeons inside took wing, and then you needed a good many guards, oracles, lawyers and sedatives to put them back into the cage.

The slightest piece of news and your soul leapt up like a naughty kid beckoned out to the street, heeding no warning, nor listening to any other probability.

The toughest part of my map was spring, I knew. I wouldn't have wanted to be released in the worst of the winter anyway. Once gloom settled into the air, the body just wanted to sleep.

But spring was an aphrodisiac.

Once spring touched the roof, yard or window, once the sun crept down from the wall, I'd be in for it, I knew.

There were clues: leaving at the end of visits had got much more hurtful as the snows receded. Certain letters were slashing tiny, yet painful wounds in my soul, like paper cuts. Hope swelled and ebbed like the daily tides competing with the sun in the yard.

We kept vacillating between, 'This could take much longer than we thought,' and 'It could be over any day!' We either clammed up as if on a condolence visit or sang our hearts out as if we'd gone fishing.

Hope's long term plans were clear as day: just as I had taken Ege round the Ulucanlar Prison Museum, one day I would guide him round the Silivri Museum, as a lesson to us all.

But the short term was less easy to guess. All the same, whenever I stumbled, a dark voice emanating from the past came and grabbed my arm: 'Hang in there, don't humiliate me!'

Celebrations – of birthdays, anniversaries, prize ceremonies, New Year's Eves and Valentine's Days – and respects to the departed, all conducted at a distance. Hearing your loved ones' tears once a week, on the ten-minute phone calls you're allowed ...

Flailing between, 'I will hold you to count for all this, for your vulgar disregard for the law, and all those refusals that came out so glibly,' and 'I will never be like you no matter what happens; I will not get angry or harbour grudges ...'

Swaying between the longing to explore those wonderful places in Cemre Birand's[433] travel book and the worry of being blown here and there in some absurd fight ...

Then, ending this internal debate with Virginia Woolf: 'You cannot find peace by avoiding life ...'

My worst fears came true in February.

The days started growing longer, it got a little warmer, and the cynical laughter of the crows was now accompanied by the first chirps of the canaries. The freshness of the buds popping outside floated in, and found me in the dungeon.

The first touch of spring on the yard splashed my heart.

Nature began turning somersaults in my blood.

The sun was now my calendar. I began to believe it brought good luck. I would be out when it came down.

By the end of January, it had come down to nearly two metres above the iron door.

By early February, I was able to stand on the chair and touch it with my tired fingers. Like a father marking his child's height, I marked its position on the wall.

Fifteen minutes, and the reluctant blonde drew its hand back… When I stepped onto the plastic chair on 13 February, it dazzled me for the first time as it shot through the wire. It touched my eyelashes and gave my eyelids a warm kiss…

Recognising the momentousness of this ritual I'd been anticipating for so long, Erdem flung open the window and the door and channelled music into the yard. Nâzım's Sunday meeting had found me on a Saturday. This was the first light of freedom. It poured into my heart from my eyes.

We flirted for about ten minutes with the sun in that stone corner. An intoxicating sun brushed over my forehead and reached all the way down to my chin. It was light, it was dreams and it was hope raining on my face…

It transported me, mixed me into rivers, made me wander in forests and meadows, and led me to smell the flowers.

As it started to rise again ten minutes later, stroking my hair, I rose on tiptoe to hang on to its touch on my skin for a little longer…

After it had gone, I was glowing as if I had sunbathed for the first time in my life.

I don't know what Saturn was up to that day, but that was

when the news that the Constitutional Court would review our petition exploded.

The sun was bigger than Saturn, after all.

36

THANKS

THE RAIN never stopped all through the night connecting the 24th to 25 February.

It lashed the roof.

At 7 a.m., I awoke with an irrepressible hope inside. The yard door wasn't yet open, but my impatience kept prodding me, 'Go, go out, now!'

That was the date set for the Constitutional Court decision.

Nothing had leaked, but I was certain of the outcome. The signs were very strong:

The sun had descended to the yard.

I'd come to the end of my notebook.

The pro-government media had gone berserk.

Spring had come.

I sat down to write my article for the day after, since I

probably wouldn't have the time at my release. It shouldn't be an outpouring of rage. The palace fed on rage. On the contrary, it had to deprive him of sustenance; a sharp-witted satire in a tone of invincibility that he dislikes so much.

It had to demonstrate that this injustice had only reinforced our resolve and increased our fame while it exposed to the whole world the crime that was being covered up. It had to be an 'attempt at cronyism' couched in faultlessly courteous terms.

I wrote *An Open Letter of Thanks to Erdoğan.*

Dear Mr President,

The whole world knows that we owe our three-month-long detention to your personal complaint and to the unquestioning obeisance of the criminal court judges who never make you ask anything twice.

I am of the view that I owe you thanks for this detention on a number of counts.

Prison was missing from my CV; thanks to you, that gap has been filled.

Liberated from a phone tapped by you, I read books I'd been intending to for a long time, wrote more than I had ever before (and wrote much more freely, now the risk of being arrested by you was gone), and worked out much more than I would have been able to outside, pacing for miles and playing ball. I got to know other people and other lives. I gathered enough material to last a writer for a lifetime. I entertained more MPs and lawyers than I had ever seen up to that point.

All this is thanks to you.

You have made it possible for me to spend a New Year's Eve in prison – and I have no idea how many more I had in store – thereby reminding me to treasure a New Year's Eve spent with my loved ones…

You have protected us from the escalating civil war situation in the land, the swine flu epidemic, air pollution and the worst of the winter by banging us up.

You have also conferred upon us the rare privilege of appreciating our popularity and feeling the support we had, something that is denied to most until they had passed on; you have triggered a great deal of attention that we neither demanded, nor indeed, merited.

Thanks to you, I was named as the Best Writer of the Year – surpassing Orhan Pamuk – even though I wrote no books last year.

You needn't have bothered.

You gave us the opportunity to demonstrate that not every journalist can be drowned in the pool, and not everyone can be bent to your will.

Please accept our sincerest gratitude…

The three months we spent in detention is nothing next

to those who have been languishing inside, stifling in solitary confinement for years, the objects of the thousands of charges of insult that you have filed; that being said, by throwing us in prison you have offered us a dais, an outlet for their voices, for which we must extend our express thanks.

As for the matter of those MİT lorries that you'd been trying to conceal from the whole world on the pretext of state secrets, and banged us up for: when you did bang us up, that news reverberated around the world from Japan through to Canada, from Oceania through to Indonesia. There can't be a single person left who hasn't heard; we cannot thank you enough for your input.

How astute of you.

And that's not all. We found the opportunity to announce to the whole world the growing authoritarianism in Turkey, the lawlessness and the danger of war. What other power could have given me the chance to write to *The Guardian*, *Der Spiegel*, the *Washington Post* and *Le Monde* all inside one month? What other power would have urged the American Vice-President to visit my family, if not your unchecked might?

Thanks to you and your hatchet men, we enjoyed the professional solidarity we'd been longing for on both national and international levels, gathered hundreds on our Vigil of Hope, enjoyed a sorely missed atmosphere of triumph at our release and sang together, boys and girls. How kind of you.

And finally, it is to your authoritarian disregard for the law that we owe the Constitutional Court's decision which effectively stated, 'Enough is enough; this is where we stand.' Yet another thing we cannot deny.

Not to complain or anything, but the mortgage is in arrears now; in the hope that you will contribute to us catching up through the compensation we will receive for our unlawful detention, I would request you to accept my gratitude.

Yours concernedly,

37

RELEASE

I WAS packing my things, stuffing jumbo-sized black bin liners with the mementos of my three-month captivity. Keeping my ears peeled for the sound of the TV downstairs all the while.

But it was Erdem's voice that came first: 'Unlawful! Unlawful they said!'

The ruling of the Constitutional Court was on TV, running on a breaking news ticker tape.

Unlike English, Turkish syntax normally places the verb last, which meant that the ruling was only revealed right at the end as the ticker tape ran, '*THE CONSTITUTIONAL COURT HAS DELIBERATED ON THE PETITION BY CAN DÜNDAR AND ERDEM GÜL ON THE MATTER OF THEIR DETENTION, WHICH IT HAS RULED AS UNLAWFUL.*' Erdem had been holding his breath all that time.

I flew downstairs the moment I heard. We hugged.

It was over.

Justice had spoken after ninety-two days and confirmed that there were judges in Ankara after all.

We were hopping and skipping like children and congratulating our imprisoners with inappropriate gestures, but refrained from going out into the yard in case we offended our neighbours.

Every channel ran the news at the same time.

I kept one ear on the news as I launched into the random activities I'd last done when I was waiting for Ege's birth: dusting the place and clearing out the cupboards. I pressed the warning button, shared the good news with the warders and asked for boxes to help with our release.

The Warden came over to congratulate us, adding the good news that we could be out of there within an hour of him receiving the order.

Silivri's impermeable corridors were redolent of the seductive perfume of freedom. We took pains not to inhale too deeply so as not to make our captive neighbours envious, but we did believe this decision would pave the way for their release too.

The hours dragged on like weeks. The news we were waiting for just wouldn't come. We were watching the scene outside the prison on Halk TV – which had required a petition and the support of journalist and CHP MP Barış Yarkadaş before it became available inside. Our friends and family were arriving. Erdem and I kept pointing them out to each other and waving at the screen.

Akın and Mustafa Kemal Güngör arrived at night and explained the release procedure. Akın reminded me not to make another announcement that might get me into trouble on our way out.

I, for my part, wanted to assert that we hadn't been poisoned by rage inside. We weren't after revenge; all we wanted was justice for everyone.

I wished that when the 'will that flung us in here' faced the court tomorrow, it wouldn't be tried in the same conditions. We would be the first to defend them should there be the slightest miscarriage of justice.

All I wanted to say was this, to remind everyone about those still inside and thank our vigil keepers. They had shown that a tiny tent could defy a gigantic palace and that a wooden chair could overturn the will of a gilded throne.

We waited with our bags piled at the door, as the Silivri gate got more and more crowded by midnight. It was around 2 a.m. when the warders finally arrived; we loaded our stuff into a handcart.

We said the customary 'God save you' to those remaining inside as we left.

We heard their 'Don't forget about us' called out from their hatches.

We boarded a white van.

We descended into a forest of friendship waiting at the gate.

It was now 26 February. Erdoğan's birthday.

It wasn't on my speech plan, but I wanted to mark it anyway.

'This release is our present to him,' I said. That's how I bade goodbye to the owner of my three-month temporary accommodation.

Hugged by the arms of my loved ones, I passed from the Silivri closed prison to the semi-open prison that is Turkey.

NOT THE END

NOTES

1. The *Hürriyet* is a mainstream secularist broadsheet.
2. Journalist, winner of the 2010 Oxfam Novib/PEN Freedom of Expression Award, charged with membership of the Ergenekon conspiracy together with Ahmet Şık.
3. *Adalet ve Kalkınma Partisi:* Justice and Development Party.
4. Award-winning journalist charged with membership of the Ergenekon conspiracy.
5. *Cumhuriyet Halk Partisi* (the People's Republican Party).
6. Pro-government columnist writing for the *Star*.
7. Head of the National Intelligence Agency, Hakan Fidan, is referred to as the 'black box' of the Republic of Turkey by Erdoğan.
8. *Neither Victims nor Executioners* (in Turkish), cited by Ahmet Cemal, Franz Kafka, *The Trial* (in Turkish), translated by Ahmet Cemal (Istanbul: Can, 2015).
9. The Armenian Secret Army for the Liberation of Armenia.

10. Brother of Deniz Gezmiş, political activist executed in 1972 for attempting to overthrow the Constitutional Order in contravention of article 146 of the TR Penal Code.

11. The Gülen movement is an Islamist organisation – perhaps more accurately described as a sect, founded by Fethullah Gülen. Initially an unofficial partner of the AKP in the Turkish government, it has since fallen out of favour. The Turkish government alleges that, despite defining itself as a civil society organisation, it is in fact involved in illegal activities within the state apparatus. There are ongoing investigations in relation to these allegations.

12. In 2007, in a series of investigations and court cases known collectively as 'Ergenekon', hundreds of individuals, including members of the armed forces, writers, lawyers and journalists, were accused of conspiring to overthrow the government. All those accused or sentenced were subsequently released, and the judicial process was shown to be flawed and some of the evidence used against them fabricated.

13. Member of the Cumhuriyet Foundation.

14. *The Risale-i Nur* is an interpretation of the Koran by Said Nursi.

15. A car crash in Susurluk led to the disclosure of the 'deep state': the close relationship between politicians, the police and organised crime.

16. A high-profile Gülenist prosecutor in the Ergenekon investigation, Öz fled to Armenia after having been disbarred and was later sought on an arrest warrant.

294

17. Sezen Aksu is a top pop musician and composer. Celalettin Can was a leading figure in the Revolutionary Youth Federation, nominated as one of the 'wise people' to assist in the peace process between Turkey and the Kurds. Mahmut Tanal was an Istanbul CHP MP of Republican People's Party in 2011.

18. 'We were made to stand at the bottom of a wall / Our likenesses were took on a blank page' from an Aegean folk song quoted in Yashar Kemal, *Memed, My Hawk* (Istanbul: Remzi, 1958).

19. Novelist and playwright Orhan Kemal (sentenced to five years in 1938) and poet Nâzım Hikmet (tried and sentenced several times between 1925 and 1938).

20. Satirist Aziz Nesin (sentenced to ten months in August 1947), author Sabahattin Ali (imprisoned and later killed on 2 April 1948), investigative journalist Uğur Mumcu (assassinated on 24 January 1993) and editor-in-chief of *Cumhuriyet* İlhan Selçuk (detained on 21 March 2008 under the now discredited Ergenekon conspiracy investigation).

21. Mahir Çayan, one of the leaders of the 1968 revolutionary generation, kidnapped the Israeli Consul-General Ephrahim Elrom and was captured on 1 June 1971. He escaped from prison on 29 October 1974.

22. Approximately £75.

23. A former member of the ultra-nationalist Grey Wolves and a notorious Mafia boss.

24. Mine Söğüt, *Kırmızı Zaman* (Istanbul: YKY, 2016).

25. Chairman of the Diyarbakır Bar Association shot in the head during armed clashes while issuing a press statement about the Four-Pillar Minaret.

26. Editor-in-chief of Turkey's main Armenian weekly *Agos*, assassinated in 2007.

27. Stefan Zweig and Anthea Bell (translator), 'A Chess Story', *The Collected Novellas of Stefan Zweig* (London: Pushkin Press, 2015).

28. Bülent Ecevit: poet and politician who served as PM of Turkey four times between 1974 and 2002 and was briefly imprisoned after the 1980 coup.

29. Mamak was the main prison after the 1980 coup, and it was alleged to offer highly comfortable conditions.

30. *Toplu Konut İdaresi:* Directorate of Housing Development.

31. Approximately 50p.

32. *Daddy, Why Are You Put There? The Truth Will Out* (in Turkish) (Istanbul: Doğan, 2012).

33. Daughter of Abdi İpekçi, the editor-in-chief of the centre-left *Milliyet,* assassinated on 1 February 1979.

34. *Our Struggle and Defence* (in Turkish) (Istanbul: Can, 2015).

35. Famous German investigative journalist.

36. Turkish edition translated by Selçuk Budak (Istanbul: Okuyan Us, 2009).

37. Viktor E. Frankl, *Man's Search for Meaning* (New York: Simon and Schuster, 1985), p. 97.

38. *I'm in Such a Place That* by Hasan Hüseyin Korkmazgil, made into a popular song by Ahmet Kaya.

39. Güldal Mumcu is the widow of Uğur Mumcu; Dolunay Kışlalı is the daughter of academic, writer and former Minister for Culture Ahmet Taner Kışlalı assassinated on 21 October 1999 and Zeynep Altıok is the daughter of poet Metin Altıok, killed in the arson attack on the Madımak Hotel on 2 July 1993.

40. *Tüm Öğretmenler Birleşme ve Dayanışma Derneği:* Society of All Teachers' Union and Solidarity.

41. Folk musician and a cheering figure during the Gezi Park protests who inspired the chant 'We're Mustafa Keser's soldiers' in a parody of 'We're Mustafa Kemal's soldiers'.

42. Julius Fučik and Celal Üster (translator), *Notes from the Gallows* (Istanbul: Yordam, 2015).

43. Journalist and wife of fellow journalist Mehmet Ali Birand.

ENGLISH PEN

FREEDOM TO **WRITE**
FREEDOM TO **READ**

"WHEN ANOTHER WRITER IN ANOTHER HOUSE IS NOT FREE, NO WRITER IS FREE. THIS, INDEED, IS THE SPIRIT THAT INFORMS THE SOLIDARITY FELT BY PEN, BY WRITERS ALL OVER THE WORLD."

ORHAN PAMUK

English PEN defends the right to freedom of expression in the UK and internationally. We champion the most exciting new literature in translation and give young people, prisoners and refugees the opportunity to discover their own creative abilities. We reward outstanding writing with annual prizes and hold literary events all year round.

Join English PEN and help promote the freedom to write and the freedom to read

www.englishpen.org